Teaching International Students

Teaching International Students explores the challenges presented to lecturer and student alike by increased cultural diversity within universities.

Packed with practical advice from experienced practitioners and underpinned by reference to pedagogic theory throughout, topics covered include:

- the issues arising from international students studying alongside 'home' students
- the nature of learning and teacher–student relationships
- curriculum and development of teaching skills
- multicultural group work
- postgraduate supervision
- the experience of the international student

Teaching International Students is essential reading. It demonstrates how improved training for teachers and a better understanding of the international student can enhance the experience of both and, ultimately, provide more positive learning environments for international students in the higher education system.

Ms Jude Carroll is a Staff and Educational Developer, Oxford Centre for Staff and Learning Development (OCSLD) at Oxford Brookes University, UK.

Dr Janette Ryan is a Senior Lecturer in Education at Monash University, Australia.

The Staff and Educational Development Series

Series editor: Professor James Wisdom

A Guide to Staff and Educational Development
Edited by Peter Kahn and David Baume

Inspiring Students
Edited by Stephen Fallows and Kemal Abmet

The Management of Independent Learning
Edited by Jo Tait and Peter Knight

Managing Educational Development Projects
Effective management for maximum impact
Edited by Carole Baume, Paul Martin and Mantz Yorke

Motivating Students
Edited by Sally Brown, Steve Armstrong and Gail Thompson

Research, Teaching and Learning in Higher Education
Edited by Peter Knight

Reshaping Teaching in Higher Education
Linking teaching with research
Edited by Alan Jenkins, Rosanna Breen and Roger Lindsay

Resource-Based Learning
Edited by Sally Brown and Brenda Smith

Teaching International Students
Edited by Jude Carroll and Janette Ryan

SEDA is the Staff and Educational Development Association. It supports and encourages developments in teaching and learning in higher education through a variety of methods: publications, conferences, networking, journals, regional meetings and research – and through various SEDA Accreditations Schemes.

SEDA
Selly Wick House
59–61 Selly Wick Road
Selly Park
Birmingham B29 7JE
Tel: 0121 415 6801
Fax: 0121 415 6802
Email: office@seda .ac.uk
Website: www.seda.ac.uk

Teaching International Students

Improving learning for all

**Edited by Jude Carroll
and Janette Ryan**

Routledge
Taylor & Francis Group

LONDON AND NEW YORK

First published 2005 by Routledge
2 Park Square, Milton Park, Abingdon, Oxon OX14 4RN

Simultaneously published in the USA and Canada
by Routledge
270 Madison Avenue, New York, NY 10016

Routledge is an imprint of the Taylor & Francis Group

Transferred to Digital Printing 2006

Typeset in Times by
GreenGate Publishing Services, Tonbridge

British Library Cataloguing in Publication Data
A catalogue record for this book is available from the
British Library

Library of Congress Cataloging in Publication Data
A catalog record for this book has been requested

ISBN10: 0-415-35065-4 (hbk)
ISBN10: 0-415-35066-2 (pbk)

ISBN13: 9-78-0-415-35065-5 (hbk)
ISBN13: 9-78-0-415-35066-2 (pbk)

Publisher's Note
The publisher has gone to great lengths to ensure the
quality of this reprint but points out that some
imperfections in the original may be apparent

Contents

Contributors

Ms Jude Carroll is a Teaching Fellow based in the Oxford Centre for Staff and Learning Development (OCSLD) at Oxford Brookes University in the United Kingdom. She has lived and worked in the US, several European countries and in Africa. She provides staff development on teaching international students to university staff across the United Kingdom. She has published in the area of plagiarism and international students and is the author of *A Handbook for Deterring Plagiarism in Higher Education* (2002).

Mr Glauco De Vita is a Principal Lecturer and a Teaching Fellow at Oxford Brookes University Business School. His research interests include the internationalisation of business education, and culturally inclusive pedagogies. He has published widely in these areas in journals such as *Studies in Higher Education*, the *Journal of Further and Higher Education*, *Assessment & Evaluation in Higher Education*, *Teaching in Higher Education*, *Active Learning in Higher Education*, *The International Journal of Management Education*, and *Innovations in Education and Teaching International*.

Ms Lee Dunn is a lecturer and academic developer in the Teaching and Learning Centre of Southern Cross University. Her areas of interest are teaching and learning in higher education, particularly the assessment of student learning. She is co-author of *The Student Assessment Handbook* (2004) and has published and spoken about transnational education, and has also taught on transnational programmes.

Dr Susan Hellmundt has lived and worked in several countries including the UK, Germany and France and speaks fluent German and French. She has extensive experience in teaching English as a second language in a wide range of contexts, both in Australia and Europe. She is an experienced educator and in the last nine years has been teaching international students in the tertiary sector in Management and Education while completing her MA in curriculum and pedagogy, and her PhD, the focus of which was curriculum internationalisation. Susan has written extensively on the issue and has presented her theoretical framework and teaching strategies to audiences across

Australia, and in the United States and the United Kingdom. Susan runs her own consultancy on teaching strategies for culturally inclusive classrooms and can be contacted via her website at www.ic-comms.com or by email to shellmun@bigpond.net.com.

Dr Betty Leask is Dean: Teaching and Learning in the Division of Business in the University of South Australia, Australia. She initiates and supports activities to promote and improve learning for all students including internationalisation of the curriculum in both Adelaide and Asia. She is also interested in the application of new technologies to teaching and learning, quality assurance, improving access for a range of equity groups and contributing to university policy development. Details of her publications and research interests are on http://people.unisa.edu.au/betty.leask.

Professor Kam Louie is Dean of Arts at the University of Hong Kong. He has written extensively on Chinese literature, philosophy and education. His books include *Theorising Chinese Masculinity* (Cambridge University Press, 2002), *The Politics of Chinese Language and Culture* (Routledge, 1998) and *Inheriting Tradition* (Oxford University Press, 1986).

Dr Patricia McLean is Director, Equity, Language and Learning Programs at the University of Melbourne, Australia. Her department includes the Language and Learning Skills Unit and in addition she has responsibility for postgraduate and undergraduate transition programmes and for equity and diversity policy and planning. Pat has worked as both an academic and an administrator in higher education and has experience teaching international students from a wide range of disciplines. Her doctorate is in the learning support needs of post-secondary students with psychiatric disabilities and current research interests are in programme evaluation and inclusive curriculum.

Ms Laurie Ransom was educated in both the United States and Australia. Laurie has an MA in Foreign Language and Literatures and a Graduate Diploma in Education in TESOL and French. Her ten years plus of language teaching has included developing targeted programmes and materials for ESL/EFL students in the United States, China and Australia. In addition to teaching, Laurie has had over eight years of management experience in the education sector, focusing on both support programmes to enhance the international student experience and also academic skills programmes for tertiary students. She has considerable experience and interest in cross-cultural teaching and learning issues and is currently managing the Language and Learning Skills Unit at the University of Melbourne, Australia.

Dr Janette Ryan is Senior Lecturer in Education at Monash University, Australia. She is the author of *A Guide to Teaching International Students* (2000) published by the Oxford Centre for Staff and Learning Development. She has researched the experiences of staff and students at universities in the

United Kingdom and Australia in relation to the teaching and learning needs of international students. Janette has been an international student in China and the United Kingdom and has taught international students at Western universities. Her doctorate was on teaching and learning for diverse groups of higher education students.

Ms Diane Schmitt is a Principal Lecturer in the School of Arts, Communication and Culture at Nottingham Trent University and head of the EFL/TESOL team. She has lived and worked in the US, Japan, Azerbaijan and the UK. For the past fourteen years, she has been teaching English for Academic Purposes to international students from a wide range of national backgrounds. Her interests lie in writing in a second language, second language acquisition and language testing. She has recently co-authored a student text entitled *Focus on Vocabulary: Mastering the Academic Word List* (2005).

Associate Professor James Sillitoe works in the Office for Postgraduate Study at Victoria University, Australia. After seventeen years as a lecturer in Applied Chemistry, James moved into the student support area of the university to work with Federal Government initiatives to increase the participation of students from non-traditional educational backgrounds in higher education. His work now includes supervising postgraduate research students and assisting beginning research students from non-traditional backgrounds to make the transition into postgraduate study. He is co-editor of *Assisting Research Students from Non-traditional Backgrounds* (2002).

Professor Graham Webb is Pro Vice-Chancellor (Quality) at Monash University. He holds the qualifications of BA Honours, MSc, PhD with distinction and PGCE. Graham has been a teacher, researcher and manager in universities for over thirty years including seven years at the University of Ulster in Ireland, six years at the University of the West Indies in Jamaica, eleven years at the University of Otago in New Zealand and seven years at Monash University. Graham is author or editor of nine books and numerous book chapters and journal articles concerning organisational and staff development, and the theory and practice of teaching and learning in higher education. He is an international consultant and chair of national academic audits.

Ms Janis Webb is a Senior Lecturer in the Student Learning Unit at Victoria University, Australia. For many years she has assisted students in the Faculty of Business and Law, many of whom are international students or students from non-English speaking backgrounds, to make the transition from undergraduate to postgraduate study. Janis is a member of the Australasian Evaluation Society, and collaborates with academic staff to design and conduct evaluations of their mainstream programmes using qualitative methodologies. She is co-editor of *Assisting Research Students from Non-traditional Backgrounds* (2002) and *Academic Skills Advising: Evaluating for*

Program Improvement and Accountability (2002). She is currently undertaking a PhD study into doctoral education in Australia.

Ms Christabel Ming Zhang is a lecturer in the School of Applied Economics at Victoria University, Australia. Christabel's initial studies for her qualification in Business and her work with tertiary Business students as a TEFL lecturer at Beijing No. 2 Foreign Language University were followed by experience as an international student at Victoria University where she obtained a Graduate Diploma in Tourism and a Master of Education (by research) at Victoria University. Christabel lectures in Economics and collaborates with the Student Learning Unit in the development of subject-specific academic skills programmes to support the transition to Australian higher education for international students.

Introduction

'Canaries in the coalmine'

International students in Western universities

Dr Janette Ryan, Monash University
Ms Jude Carroll, Oxford Brookes University

Higher education (HE) institutions in English-speaking countries now contain a more socially and culturally diverse student population than ever before, including increasing numbers of international students. Such changes present challenges for teachers in higher education, especially as increasing workloads add further pressures. In this book, we speak of 'international students' when we mean students who have chosen to travel to another country for tertiary study. They may or may not have attended some secondary or preparatory education in the country they have selected for higher education but most of their previous experience will have been of other educational systems, in cultural contexts and sometimes in a language that is different (or very different) from the one in which they will now study. We also speak of 'home students', meaning those who have chosen to remain in the country where they attended secondary school or had their prior educational experiences. In this book, the authors concentrate on issues arising in programmes delivered in the home country (termed 'on-shore' in Australia) where the numbers of international students can range from just one or two to a significant majority. Off-shore programmes, where universities deliver their own programmes in other countries, bring their own set of challenges; many of the themes and activities discussed in this book will also apply in off-shore teaching although this is not the primary focus.

This first chapter outlines the issues arising from having many more international students studying alongside home students in on-shore programmes at tertiary level. Later chapters focus on specific aspects of teaching international students, offering practical suggestions and exploring how greater diversity affects the nature of learning and knowledge and relationships between teachers and learners. The final section of the book considers the curriculum, suggests how to develop teachers' skills and reminds readers thinking about teaching of the experiences of international students themselves.

Imperatives for change: changing students

In 2000/2001, 11 per cent of higher education students in the United Kingdom and 13 per cent of higher education students in Australia were international students (with similar levels in many European countries). The figure was 3 per cent in the United States (totalling approximately half a million students), 3 per cent in Canada, and 5 per cent in New Zealand (UNESCO, 2003). By 2004, the numbers in the UK had increased to 16 per cent of full-time students (HESA, 2005) and in Australia in 2005 to 24 per cent (DEST, 2005). Countries like the United States and the United Kingdom have long traditions of welcoming students from overseas, but in some other countries, such changes are a relatively recent phenomenon.

National statistics such as those quoted above cannot capture the impact of local changes in individual HE institutions in English-speaking countries such as the US, UK, Australia, Canada and New Zealand, nor do they show how dramatically some national HE systems have changed. For example, statistics in the UK for students arriving from outside the European Union show.

1995   fewer than 100,000 non-EU students
2001/2   just over 150,000 non-EU students
2004   almost 195,000 non-EU students

(HESA, 2005)

The trend is, if anything, predicted to accelerate. Comparable figures for Australia predict that the 2003 levels (303,324 students) will rise to 810,000 by 2018 (IDP Australia, 2004).

Another aspect of the large increases in the numbers of international students is the more diverse skill range of the students who travel to study. In many ways, the issues surrounding international students mirror the experience of widening participation per se. In the past, students from many countries found it difficult or impossible to access Western universities because governments and scholarship providers vetted students then selected the elite few who, in their view, deserved support and were likely to succeed. Now, university entrance requirements, the student's own financial resources, and the wish to access higher education are the only (though sometimes challenging) limiting factors for students wishing to study in other countries.

All indications are that more and more students will choose to travel to Western universities in future. Looking to Australia as one example, it has been estimated that the numbers of international students will increase sevenfold by 2025. The British Council predicts 677,000 students will travel to the UK to study by 2015 and 1,330,000 by 2025 (British Council, 2005). The economic benefits of increasing numbers of international students are well known (Johnes, 2004), but there have been debates about the quality of higher education provision and outcomes for the students themselves. Such issues need to be tackled quickly so that universities' reputations, the experience of all students, and the morale of those who teach them are not damaged.

Changing needs and expectations

The increased numbers of international students in Western universities bring challenges for lecturers and international students alike. Many lecturers, faced with unfamiliar student characteristics and needs, are unsure how to respond whilst at the same time meeting what they perceive to be the academic expectations of the institution for research, new programme development and/or income generation. Such tensions can lead to ad hoc decisions by individual lecturers and a 'lottery' system for students as to how well their needs are met. Lecturers can feel that they are constantly 're-inventing the wheel' when in fact their colleagues are facing similar dilemmas. It is easiest, often, for lecturers to stick to their existing assumptions about and expectations of the 'ideal student'.

Many international students, too, face significant difficulties. Having taken the decision to study abroad, many encounter difficulties in their quest to be academically successful in their new learning environment. Home students also find the transition to higher education taxing until they become accustomed to academic language and conventions, independent learning and class participation. Even students with a good command of English can struggle with local language peculiarities and lack of discipline-specific vocabulary. However, international students must deal with all these things and more: they face different social and cultural mores and customs, norms and values from the ones they have known; different modes of teaching and learning; and different expectations and conventions about participation and performance. They often bring with them acute awareness of the high expectations family and friends have for their success. They must cope without their usual support systems, and have the added pressure of visa implications for any academic failure. Often, each problem exacerbates the others and can become overwhelming, leading to considerable stress and even mental health disorders.

The challenge, then, becomes addressing the needs of both teachers and international students within the context of higher education becoming ever more pressurised and resource constrained. We assert that the answer does not lie in doing more but rather in viewing the problem differently, in doing different things, and in thinking creatively about the major issues which underpin concerns about teaching the ever larger number of international students we encounter in our classrooms.

Responding to changes

Any reassessment of current teaching practice for many teachers may need to start with how they see international students as learners. The authors of this book all start with the premise that international students arrive with a set of skills and experiences which have equipped them in the past to be successful but which may not be fully useful in their new setting. This has not been the tone of much of the literature on teaching international students (nor of much of the discussion you might hear in staff common rooms when international students are discussed by lecturers). Often, a deficit view of international students sees them as lacking in independent, critical thinking skills; as plagiarisers or rote learners, speaking broken English and having awkward ways of participating in class. Yet when examined, the deficit model is hard to sustain. International students have been successful in their home countries and have shown enterprise and initiative in trying to succeed in a foreign environment, often in a foreign and inherently difficult language. It is all too easy to overlook these positive attributes when dealing with students who don't have the background knowledge and experiences that we assume of our students or who don't yet possess the sophisticated language needed to express ideas and demonstrate their abilities. We often hear or read clumsy English and misinterpret this as clumsy thinking. We see plagiarism where we may not have noticed it among local students. We equate language skills and confident styles with intelligence and the results of hard work. In our busy lives, and usually frantic assessment periods, we generally do not have the time and patience to look beyond style for the substance and understanding.

The contributors to this book would argue that there is another way, though the rhetoric of diversity often does not translate easily into practice. The structure of this book arose from the authors' experiences with rethinking our own teaching to seek to be more inclusive, from our own experiences of being cross-cultural travellers ourselves, and from ideas gathered in our own specific expertise in areas of professional interest. Between us, we have lived, worked or studied in Africa, America, Asia, Australasia and Europe, gathering experiences that have shaped our world-views and our intellectual beliefs and academic practices. Although not always easy, we believe that these experiences have enriched and continue to enrich our teaching and learning practices.

The basic premise that we, the authors, have taken in this book on teaching international students is that by adopting approaches that are inclusive of international students, we will also be more generally inclusive of a broader range of learners. Students with little family experience of higher education, mature students, students with disabilities, students from disadvantaged backgrounds and indigenous students may face difficulties which are similar to those described in this book. By adopting approaches that are culturally inclusive of international students, we will also be more generally inclusive, operating within a framework where the needs of teachers and students can be addressed and included.

How this book is structured

Part I begins by considering underpinning cultural beliefs and theories of cultural migration as they impact on learning. It begins by suggesting ways in which teachers can unlock and use the experiences, knowledge and cultural beliefs students bring with them into the classroom. In this section and in other chapters throughout the book, we consider what an academic culture might be and how to help students adapt what previously worked well to fit the new context. Nearly everyone has heard of culture shock but few talk about the equally difficult 'academic shock' students experience when their confidence plummets, they question their previous self-evaluation as competent learners, and they may even lose their knowledge about how to learn and succeed. Many people, the authors included, know from their own international experiences the frustrations of attempting to explain our ideas or express our personalities in a foreign language or where it was not clear what was expected. Chapter 2 considers how best to discover and use the cultural capital all students bring with them to the classroom.

Continuing the theme of cross-cultural knowledge and its impact on learning, Chapter 3 alerts us to the rewards and dangers of making assumptions about others' experiences and cultures. Chapter 4 explores the idea of explicitness – of the need to make clear the rules of the new game – in many different contexts. Here, the emphasis is on the idea of an academic culture per se and the fact that each of us has our own assumptions and behaviours that will probably be different (or very different) from the academic culture(s) our international students bring to the classroom. Rather than seeing the higher education models in Western countries as 'normal' and international students as strange, lecturers who are aware of their own beliefs can, if they wish, consider how their rules and beliefs might be explained and taught to those who do not yet understand them. Chapter 4 offers specific suggestions for identifying your own academic cultural beliefs and assumptions with a view to sharing them with your students. Chapter 5 specifically addresses issues linked to learning in English as a second (or even third or fourth) language.

Inclusive teaching also means adopting a range of methods and activities in a range of settings. Part II suggests teaching methods appropriate to all students and especially welcomed by international students. Chapter 6 offers practical, realistic suggestions for helping students develop the academic skills they will need to be successful. Chapter 7 considers the difficult matter of student writing. Chapters 8 and 9 consider the opportunities and difficulties that come with asking students to work in multicultural groups. In Chapter 8, the author explores the overarching issues and recommends ways of making the students' cultural diversity part of the group's task. In Chapter 9, the same issues are explored when the task is rooted in the subject itself and where international students and home students, working together, must address learning within their discipline. The specific needs of postgraduate students are addressed in Chapter 11 and finally, Chapter 10 outlines best practice recommendations for modes of teaching such as lectures, seminars and tutorials derived from systematic review of the research into teaching international students, and finally, the specific needs of postgraduate students are addressed in Chapter 11.

The final section of this book, Part III, takes a broader view by focusing on issues linked to the curriculum and what we teach and research. Chapter 12 has an institutional perspective, discussing why and how institutions might internationalise their curriculum. Chapter 13 looks at the same issues at the level of individual teachers and courses. Chapter 14 considers the impact of a significant number of international students on a department's postgraduate culture and research activity.

Chapter 15 discusses ways of developing the skills of individual teachers and of institutions as a whole, using a range of strategies such as networking and formal training workshops. The final chapter, Chapter 16, returns to the experiences of students themselves, reminding readers who are focusing on teachers' concerns and experiences that students, too, are reacting to and shaping the issues discussed in this book.

Providing high-quality outcomes

As already stated, increasing numbers of international students can prompt teachers to think about how they teach, what they teach, and how to use students' previous learning experiences. Clearly, we the authors think this is an opportunity but we are well aware that others see it as a threat. We often hear colleagues worrying about lowering standards for all or having different standards for one group of students. Some talk of simply avoiding the harder skills and ideas in their teaching for fear that some students will not be able to cope. Yet by helping international students to be on an equal footing with other students, by helping them to learn and demonstrate their ability in appropriate ways, we do not need to lower standards. Indeed, international students are often amongst our highest achievers once they 'learn the rules' and there is little difference in their progress rates (DEST, 2004). But we will need to do things differently.

Alternatives should be no less rigorous and assessment criteria must still be met, but we can make decisions about, for example, the type of assessment tasks we set or the ways in which students show they have met the criteria. Perhaps we can rethink the timing of tasks to remove unnecessary barriers that disadvantage international students. We might make special efforts to find a text that covers the material but does so in a clear, accessible way. We might make sure assessment briefs are clear and easily understood. Or we could rethink the real importance of English language facility in a particular assignment. At times, the ability to use English correctly can be a legitimate assessment criterion if English proficiency is a required learning outcome. Where it is not or where students have not yet developed language facility, careful thought about the relative importance of English is not 'going easy' but rather a means of not disadvantaging some students. This is not to say we ignore English. Our international students themselves would not thank us for this as developing good language skills is often a motivation that international students have in choosing to study overseas. Also, ignoring language difficulties in the early stages of their study is unhelpful because problems with English, if ignored, generally give way to deeper difficulties of a more academic nature as the course progresses and the student must negotiate his or her way through more advanced and complex academic requirements. But we might not treat all students the same.

Making adjustments is not the same as conferring advantage. It is more about levelling the playing field so all students are doing equally difficult tasks. We need to consider in all of our teaching and learning practices and requirements who are we advantaging and who are we disadvantaging. Indirect discrimination occurs when a requirement is by its very nature harder for one group of students to achieve than for others. These imperatives need to be borne in mind when considering alternate ways of teaching and assessing students.

Challenges and rewards: bearers of culture, not bearers of problems

The presence of increased numbers of international students presents opportunities to re-assess not just how we teach but also the role and functions of the university as an institution. The presence of international students, with their diverse paradigms and life experiences, provides us with an opportunity to ask who the university is there to serve and to what end. Are we as teachers in universities custodians of convention and a defined body of wisdom, or do we believe that we have a duty to forge new traditions and epistemologies? Is our role transformative or reproductive?

We can (and many do) see international students as part of an unwelcome, commercially driven change to our working environment, adding to the demands of our already stressful and pressured lives. Or we can embrace change and welcome international students as bearers of alternative knowledge, perspectives and life experiences. Because our classrooms are more diverse, we and our local students can learn more about how to operate in culturally diverse environments. This is important not just in an increasingly global world but also because countries like the United Kingdom, the United States, Australia, Canada and New Zealand are increasingly multicultural themselves. They will need citizens who can operate successfully in this diversity. International students can (if we encourage them to do so) help home students to become global learners, competent in intercultural communication and understanding.

'Canaries in the coalmine': benefits for all

The transformation of our universities has left many issues in its wake. Such major transformations, mirroring but also driving broader social change, leave behind many dilemmas at the 'coalface' for both lecturers and students. The resolution of these issues requires soul-searching and re-adjustment, something that sits uneasily with busy schedules and multiple demands. This book explores these dilemmas and attempts to offer suggestions for new paradigms and new solutions. They are intended to relieve, not increase, the burden on higher education lecturers.

One analogy we, the authors of this chapter, both use often when thinking and talking about international students is to see them as 'canaries in the mine', harking back to the time when coalminers took canaries into mines to monitor air quality. If the canaries died, they knew that the atmosphere threatened the miners' well-being, too. We are also at a 'coalface'. The international student 'canaries' thankfully show us their difficulties in less dramatic ways but nevertheless point out aspects of our teaching that all students will probably experience as challenges.

By paying attention, we can change conditions to make sure that everyone can thrive in the higher education environment. If we improve conditions for international students, we improve them for all learners.

References

British Council (2005). www.britcoun.org/ecs/news/2003

Department of Education, Employment and Training (Australia). (2005). Selected higher education statistics. Online at www.dest.gov.au/sectors/higher_education/publications_resources/statistics/default.htm.

Department of Education, Science and Training. (2004). International higher education students: How do they differ from other higher education students? Strategic Analysis and Evaluation Group Research Note No. 2. Accessed 10 June 2004 at www.dest.gov.au/research/publications/research_notes/2.htm.

HESA (Higher Education Statistics Agency). (2005). *Students in Higher Education Institutions 2002/3* (Re-issue) Cheltenham: Higher Education Statistics Agency.

IDP Australia (2004). *International Students in Australian Universities, Semester 1, 2004, National Overview.* Sydney, NSW: IDP Education Australia.

Johnes, G. (2004). *The Global Value of Education and Training Exports to the UK Economy*, British Council online at www.britishcouncil.org/global-value-of-education and training-exports-to-the-uk-economy.pdf.

UNESCO (2003). *Global Education Digest: Comparing Education Statistics Across the World.* Montreal: UNESCO Institute for Statistics.

Part I

Cultural migration and learning

Maximising international students' 'cultural capital'

Dr Janette Ryan, Monash University
Dr Susan Hellmundt

This chapter examines the ways that lecturers can create learning contexts to assist international students to adjust to new learning environments. In order to create these contexts, we need to understand some of the underlying reasons for the difficulties that international students can face in unfamiliar academic environments. Insights gained can, in turn, guide adjustments to teaching and learning practices to better meet students' needs. Using sociocultural theories of learning, this chapter explains how students' perceptions of what is expected in higher education environments are influenced by existing understandings and epistemologies, then argues for ways of teaching that do not disadvantage and/or marginalise students coming from different social and cultural backgrounds. These strategies are described in more detail in later chapters; here, the focus is on teachers as cultural mediators, opening up a dialogue between themselves and their students.

How learning occurs: construction of knowledge

Constructivist theories of learning place the individual at the centre of the learning process. Learning is not passively received through the 'telling' of information by others, but is actively built, or constructed, by the learner (Piaget, 1959). The basis for constructivism is 'schema' theory which describes how learners' mental structures, the 'schemas' (or schemata), are used to organise knowledge. Schemas mediate experiences and channel thinking by structuring the selection, retention and use of information (Cole, 1996), summing up what we already know from previous experiences, interactions, and beliefs. New experiences can trigger modifications and over time, our schemas become both increasingly complex and sophisticated and more rooted in the social and cultural contexts in which they occur. For example, our mental schema of 'football' will depend on the particular type of football with which we are familiar, and the social and cultural forms of these experiences of football. Our schema of 'football' will change as we experience different situations in relation to the phenomenon and will be influenced by cultural factors such as the geographical area in which we reside and by social factors such as our personal, shared or vicarious experiences of football. Language, too, becomes more and more contextual. For example, the phrase 'Anne broke a bottle on the ship' will conjure up a very different schema from 'Princess Anne broke a bottle on the ship' in those familiar with conventions about royalty and the launching of ships. Those with no such background information and experiences may not conjure up two very different scenarios.

In order for new information to be understood, it has to 'hook' into existing categories of knowledge. In a constructivist view of learning, lecturers create the contexts and provide relevant information; learners, in turn, activate their existing schemas and connect them to new knowledge, thereby developing further understandings. Because learning is individually constructed, socially supported, and culturally mediated, learners in unfamiliar social and cultural environments may have difficulty in activating, or 'hooking' into, their existing schemas in order to build new knowledge, especially where new information is incongruent. The result can be 'cognitive dissonance' or psychological confusion.

Significant dissonance helps to explain the academic shock experienced by many international students, many of whom will have seen themselves as academically very successful. Often, it is more about the cultural 'distance' between the learners' previous and current contexts rather than learners' previous geographical location per se (Ninnes, Aitchison and Kalos, 1999). Whilst such reactions can be common for a whole range of learners new to higher education, they can be overwhelming for international students as they struggle with a new culture in general and an academic culture in particular. Whatever the cause, the result can be feelings of exclusion and alienation, perhaps damaging self-esteem and further hindering the learning process.

Inclusion or exclusion?

Much of the earlier literature on dealing effectively with international students stressed the need for the student to adapt as quickly as possible to 'our' academic tradition (Ballard and Clanchy, 1997) and often saw the differences between students as a deficit (Fox, 1996) with the stress on remediating the skills that international students appeared to be lacking, such as critical thinking. Other scholarship has moved away from a focus on difference and stresses instead the need for creating contexts where students can understand their new situation (Biggs, 1997) and where teachers and all students can value different ways of thinking and learning. Fox (1996) argues that intercultural dialogue provides 'the critical process of making meaning, of shared meanings, and of building bridges across those multiple realities and multiple truths' (Fox, 1996: 298). By providing the connections required by learners, by recognising potential gaps in knowledge and understanding and by attempting to explicitly fill these gaps, it is possible to see 'cognitive dissonance' as an opportunity for new learning. Bourdieu (1984) describes the social and cultural knowledge students bring as their 'cultural capital' and advocates using it to drive learning. Interactions between teachers and learners, and between learners and other learners such as those in tutorials or seminars, can allow learners to activate their 'schemas' and adjust them to the new information and insights to which they are being exposed. This adjustment can be just as significant a learning opportunity for home students and for lecturers as it is for international students. These interactions facilitate a higher level of engagement in learning and the development of more complex understandings for all learners. International students therefore need to be afforded full rights to participation and success in the classroom, in order for them to learn effectively and for others to learn effectively from them.

This view fits well with a student-centred approach where space is negotiated for all voices to be heard and listened to. The different ways of thinking and knowing are included rather than the voice of the dominant group favoured to the marginalisation of the 'Other'. The dichotomy of us and the 'Other' is not accepted. Such an agenda creates spaces for personal and professional transformation where there is a shift from student as subject to student as co-researcher with an awareness of who is speaking and who is listening. Knowing that someone is listening seriously is just as important as telling the story.

Such an approach indicates that the role of lecturers is to create a context of inclusion where interaction among international and local students is encouraged and seen in terms of promoting critical and intercultural learning opportunities (Volet and Ang, 1998). The learning context is one where student-centred activities and discussion are considered to be appropriate and assignments are structured so that all students develop critical and analytical skills. By contrast, students often take a surface approach to their learning when teaching is conceptualised as being about what the lecturers do and where their role is to transmit knowledge that has to be memorised and reproduced in exams. A context of inclusion, on the other hand, conceptualises teaching and learning as being about interaction and changing one's conceptions, and encourages a deeper approach to learning and personal transformation.

Lecturers' own assumptions about teaching and learning

For lecturers, this means that it is important not to make assumptions about the way students learn because of their cultural background or even the way they look, though this is often easier said than done. We all take short cuts when we teach or interact with students. Perhaps we refer to students 'from South East Asia' rather than recognising the variety of their social, political, linguistic, or cultural backgrounds. Perhaps we assume that all students will understand the meaning of a story or metaphor rather than explaining the meaning. But by understanding the nexus between what teachers do and how students learn, we can think about how contexts can change to better support students' learning. It is not possible for lecturers to understand the previous cultural experiences or expectations of all of their international students, although it is important to have an empathetic and sensitive approach. Lecturers need to create the contexts for students to see that it is appropriate to be included and participate in class discussion and activities (Wallace and Hellmundt, 2003).

Culturally diverse classrooms can provide a host of opportunities to promote critical thinking and intercultural communication skills for both international and local students. Strategies that promote intercultural interaction can provide students with a rich learning environment where students develop the skills to communicate in multicultural environments as well as broaden their appreciation of global understandings of knowledge. The promotion of intercultural interaction requires a range of teaching and learning strategies involving curriculum content, pedagogy and assessment techniques. These are described in more detail in later chapters in this book.

References

Ballard, B. and Clanchy, J. (1997). *Teaching Students from Overseas*. Melbourne: Longman Cheshire.

Biggs, J. (1997). 'Teaching across and within cultures'. *Learning and Teaching in Higher Education: Advancing International Perspectives, Proceedings of the HERDSA conference*, Adelaide, South Australia, 8–11 July 1997.

Bourdieu, P. (1984). *Distinction: A Social Critique of Judgement of Taste*. Cambridge, Massachusetts: Harvard University Press.

Cole, M. (1996). *Cultural Psychology: A Once and Future Discipline*. Cambridge, Massachusetts: Harvard University Press.

Fox, C. (1996). 'Listening to the other. Mapping intercultural communication in postcolonial educational consultancies'. In R. Paulston (ed.) *Social Cartography. Mapping Ways of Seeing Social and Educational Change* (pp. 291–306). New York and London: Garland Publishing Inc.

Ninnes, P., Aitchison, C. and Kalos, S. (1999). 'Challenges to stereotypes of international students' prior educational experience: Undergraduate education in India'. *Higher Education Research and Development*, 18 (3), 323–342.

Piaget, J. (1959). *The Language and Thought of the Child*. London: Routledge & Kegan Paul.

Volet, S. and Ang, G. (1998). 'Culturally mixed groups on international campuses: an opportunity for intercultural learning'. *Higher Education Research and Development*, 17 (1), 5–24.

Wallace, M. and Hellmundt, S. (2003). *Strategies for collaboration and internationalisation in the classroom*. Nurse Education in Practice 3, 1–6.

3

Gathering cultural knowledge

Useful or use with care?

Professor Kam Louie,
University of Hong Kong

Many teachers of international students seek brief, straightforward information about the students they are asked to teach. How do Korean students interact with their teachers and fellow students? How do students from the Middle East regard their sporting heroes? What topics of conversation are considered impolite for Scandinavians? Teachers who ask such questions are gathering knowledge about their students' cultures, in the hope that this cultural knowledge will make them better instructors. Before I discuss the merits and methods of gathering cultural knowledge, I should state that teachers who show genuine curiosity about their students' backgrounds are already well on the way to being better mentors. Far too often, the flow of cultural knowledge in teacher–learner relationships is seen as a one-way business. Teachers who gather cultural knowledge at the same time as they are imparting it are aware of the processes of learning about another culture, and that awareness deepens their rapport with the students.

Yet, the individual 'facts' gathered from students' cultures may not necessarily represent a true picture of the students' home environments. On the contrary, they could reflect stereotypes that are blatantly untrue, even though these stereotypes may function as a common vocabulary that bonds the teacher and student. While this function is useful in terms of the promotion of solidarity in the classroom, I aim in this chapter to show that gathering cultural knowledge in a piecemeal fashion is inefficient and the understanding created could be based on falsehoods. I propose a more general approach: while it is helpful to gather bits and pieces of cultural knowledge, in the end, it is one's attitude and empathy towards the whole idea of cultural difference that matters. Using teachers' interaction with students from Confucian-heritage cultures (CHC) as an example, this chapter will address the complex issues involved in gathering and using 'facts' about other cultures and the dangers of oversimplification and stereotyping. I argue that the best method to successful culture work is in developing a meta-cultural sensitivity and awareness.

CHC is used here to refer to cultures in East Asia such as those found in China, Taiwan, Singapore, Hong Kong, Japan and Korea. Interactions with CHC students are used as a case study because these students constitute one of the largest groups of international students from a non-Western culture who study in anglophone countries such as the UK and Australia. Also, Confucianism has undergone some of the most drastic transformations in recent decades, so that while many people continue to eulogise its virtues, these virtues are often no more than values and beliefs that have lost all currency in their host countries. Educational pronouncements based on such doubtful premises should clearly be used with care. Confucian virtues are ideal for our purposes precisely because of the bitter controversies about their utility and very existence in both their host countries and foreign lands.

Because so many East Asians have in quick succession denounced or embraced Confucianism in recent years (the most tumultuous examples being the 1973–74 anti-Confucius Movement in China and the 'New Confucian' revival in East Asia in the 1980s), it provides us a perfect case for exploring the 'how' aspects of gathering cultural knowledge. The interpretations and evaluations of the contents and values attached to a culture could change beyond recognition in a very short time. In order to attain the skills for coping with cultural changes, teachers must engage in reflecting about the whole notion of 'culture' in general, and about their own cultures in particular. As well as recognising that most cultures are in flux and that what people tell us about their own cultures is often contradicted by other informants from the same culture, teachers should also be aware that what they teach about their own cultures can often be superficial and downright misleading. Just as the most insightful and telling ideas of cultures that we try to understand are often told by 'insiders' who are most critical of their own cultures, so dynamic exchanges with students are possibly best attained when the teacher is also engaged in critically examining his/her own culture.

One of the best ways of doing this is to stand back and look at one's culture from the 'outside'. That is, to live in another culture for an extended period of time (like the students). By joining the ranks of the 'cross-cultural travellers', the teacher should be in a much better position to develop an intercultural or meta-cultural awareness that is so essential to an empathetic understanding of different cultures. Of course, not all teachers have the luxury to live in a foreign country for a year or two at will. Fortunately, an alternative to 'cross-cultural travel' is possible for teachers in a classroom with international students. This chapter targets teachers in this environment. I will explore the issues of changes in cultural norms, dynamic interactions between teachers and students, and meta-cultural sensitivity. I will then indicate how these changes affect methods used by teachers to gather cultural knowledge.

What is culture?

Before we examine methods of gathering cultural knowledge, we should be clear exactly what it is that we are attempting to gather. That is, we must ask: what is culture? When I taught a course called 'Introduction to Western Culture' in Hong Kong in the 1970s, the content of the course was based on the Great Tradition: Greek and Roman philosophies, mythologies, art and architecture, etc. and their alleged renaissance in early modern Europe. Yet it was clear that the students themselves were interested in the more mundane forms of Western culture such as dating etiquette, dress codes, and rock and roll. And their knowledge and appreciation of Western youth culture was in many ways superior to mine despite the fact that I had lived in Australia for the previous twenty years. With the rapid Westernisation of East Asia since the 1970s, I am sure that the grasp of Western (American) popular culture by the young in Hong Kong, indeed by their peers the world over, is even firmer now.

Prior to the 1970s, academic discourse generally understood 'culture' as that encapsulated in the course contents of university classes. Such highbrow approaches have changed dramatically in the last three decades. These changes are manifested with the advent of Cultural Studies as a respectable and popular academic discipline. 'Culture' has been 'democratised' so that popular culture such as pulp fiction, rap and pop art are seen as cultural artifacts to be taken seriously. When it comes to us gathering different aspects of the 'culture' of the international students, it is even more important to be clear exactly which parts of the culture we are targeting. Is learning to dance like Zorba the Greek as useful a culture-gathering exercise as reading Plato? Being a brilliant Classics professor may not necessarily help the teacher understand why Greek or Italian students like particular kinds of music or humour. This seems obvious, yet as I will show in the next section, when less familiar cultures (for Europeans) such as East Asian ones are considered, the distinctions of elite and popular, old and new, etc. are often not taken into consideration when dealing with students.

While abstract values generated by different societies are often taken as cultural values espoused and followed by these societies (for example, the controversies surrounding 'Asian values' in the 1980s and 1990s), these values need to be closely examined in order to reveal the extent to which they are still relevant. The trouble with traditional elite values is that they are often ones the younger generations (students) no longer accept or recognise. Instead of trying to find unique features of different societies, it is better to approach the task by seeing all human beings as having varying degrees of particular personality traits. This approach may not yield exotic cultural products that one could gather, but it may provide an understanding of 'culture' with which to look at people from different backgrounds.

Geert Hofstede's analysis (1980) of a survey of over 100,000 employees of IBM in forty different countries is one of the most significant studies using this approach. In this influential study, Hofstede found that the cultural dimensions of 'power distance', 'individualism-collectivism', 'masculinity-femininity', and 'uncertainty avoidance' form a generalised framework that could be used to chart the general characteristics of societies, though not necessarily each individual member of a society. In 1987, a group of researchers called 'The Chinese Culture Connection' sought to examine the universality of Hofstede's classification system. They concluded that the four dimensions are important and useful. However, they also constructed a further dimension, 'Confucian work dynamism', which encompasses elements found in the teachings of Confucius, such as persistence and perseverance, observing status distinctions, and valuing thrift. Later, Hofstede and other researchers adopted this dimension in addition to the first four in order to cater for what he calls the 'Eastern mind' as opposed to the 'Western mind' (Hofstede, 1997: 159–174).

High culture and low culture: the CHC case

The 1980s and 1990s were a time when Confucian education and the Confucian work ethic were claimed as the cause of the 'East Asian Economic Miracle'. From being attacked as the biggest obstacle to modernisation in the previous two decades, Confucianism was revived and exalted as a humane and effective vehicle for achieving modernity. Hofstede's agreement to include 'Confucian dynamism' as a fifth dimension of the human mind was part of that trend. Thus, in education, Confucian thinking was reinterpreted to show that it was most suited to modern pedagogical practices. For example, in the well-researched book *The Chinese Learner: Cultural, Psychological, and Contextual Influences,* one of the early chapters under the heading 'Setting the Scene' outlines conceptions of learning in the Confucian tradition. It is a fairly standard essay that approaches the topic typical of attempts to set 'the cultural context for Chinese learners'. The author of this chapter, Lee Wing On, agrees with studies that show that 'Asian students are not only diligent, but they also have high achievement motivation. Invariably they have a high regard for education', and he 'aims to uncover what underlies Asian people's positive attitude towards education, their achievement motivations, and their willingness to spend most of their free time in pursuit of study' (Lee, 1996: 25). Lee believes, as do most commentators, that the answer to this quest lies in Confucianism, which is explained by him as the belief in educability and perfectibility for all, learning for self-improvement and so on. While Lee is aware that elaborating Confucian ideas of education as explanations of the Asian students' love for learning may lead to overgeneralisations, what is remarkable about his assumptions and methods is that he does not question whether Asian students really 'invariably have a high regard for education'.

I have taught hundreds of Asian students, and I must say some of them do have a high regard for education. But many don't. If the teacher begins his/her classes assuming that his/her CHC students respect education, what is s/he to think when a particular Singaporean student regards studying as a waste of time, a Vietnamese student resents being told s/he should study harder or a Taiwanese student spends all his/her time playing baseball rather than study? Not only can one be wrong about one's students from another culture, but more importantly, the stereotyping of that culture can also mislead one into classroom interactions that are just culturally inappropriate. Thus, using Lee's essay as an example again, we find that he cites ideas from classical philosophers such as Mencius and Xunzi as well as contemporary thinkers such as the Harvard-based neo-Confucianist Tu Wei-ming and Columbia University emeritus Wm. Theodore de

Bary to substantiate his claim that Confucian education stands for self-cultivation, egalitarian ideals, reflective thinking and so on. These are people who lived thousands of years apart temporally and thousands of miles apart spatially. Their contexts cannot be more different. Yet, Lee, as most scholars who write on this topic, treats Confucian education for the last two thousand years as an essential thing that remains more or less the same. This is similar to treating Christianity as the same in all places and times.

It is not difficult for teachers to see that their own countries have changed very dramatically in the last two or three decades. But many do not see (not having lived there) how even more dramatically CHC countries have changed. Each year, these countries physically change beyond recognition, so much so that even the superficial physical transformations have many of their own citizens feeling dazed and lost in the new landscape. Social and cultural transformations are occurring at an even more profound level and rapid rate. But if their own people are not aware of physical changes that are visible, it is even less possible for them to be aware of attitudinal changes that are subtle though fundamental. Many of us living in Christian countries know that the Seventh Day Adventists, Mormons, Quakers and Ku Klux Klan represent very different (and non-mainstream) brands of Christianity. None can be said to be the only true Christian belief. Yet, in the classroom, difference is most visible by their extreme representations, as the common perception of Muslims as Islamic fundamentalists shows. In the same way, East Asian students are, thanks to the writings of neo-Confucian philosophers, often seen in stereotypical ways such as having respect for learning and having filial feelings for the teacher.

When is knowing culture 'knowing'?

As I have shown elsewhere (Louie, 1986; Louie, 2002: 42–57), in the last century, interpretations of Confucianism, particularly that of Confucian education, have undergone transformations that have at times rendered any commonly accepted interpretation meaningless. And we must also remember that 'commonly accepted' could mean an interpretation embraced by the traditional Chinese scholar, the Communist cadre or the Western liberal Sinologist. By the same token, what are seen as stereotypes are only stereotypes belonging to certain groups of people in specific times and places. Thus, while self-cultivation is accepted as a major tenet of Confucian education by neo-Confucianists, some are now reinterpreting Confucian education as a path to wealth and democracy. Such a view would have been considered outrageous heresy by any traditional Confucian. It is clear that like other great figures such as Christ and the Buddha, Confucius' thinking could be twisted to suit all times and needs. Thus, on page 34 of Lee Wing On's paper, John Biggs is cited as arguing that Confucius saw himself as a deep learner. The idea that Confucianism encourages deep teaching and learning processes is in fact the most interesting and perhaps not 'commonly accepted' view in Lee's essay.

The idea is based on John Biggs' observation that CHC students are 'deep' learners rather than surface learners and, tracing this learning approach back to the teachings of Confucius, Lee makes use of the very important and influential work of people like Biggs who had successfully challenged the long-held Western beliefs that CHC learners are passive, compliant and prone to rote learning so that their understandings of matters at hand are superficial and mechanical. These beliefs have been so prevalent and entrenched that even the CHC students themselves have often internalised these descriptions of themselves and accept the image of themselves as lacking in initiative, socially inept and boringly bookish. Western teachers by contrast have also internalised the notion that their own personalities and cultures are assertive, independent-minded and better skilled socially. Indeed, some researchers such as Ballard and Clanchy (1997) use the term 'deficit' to describe the learning capacities of the students. Such ideologies only strengthen the practice of a one-way flow of knowledge from teachers to students. This practice does little to encourage productive two-way interaction between the teachers and students.

Scholars such as Biggs have therefore performed an extremely important and necessary service to the practice of teaching CHC students in debunking the 'deficit' model. However, it must be remembered that while it is refreshing to have the stereotypes of Asian students as ineffective rote learners challenged and negated, we must always be mindful that we do not go to the other extreme and see a once maligned educational system as a born-again new saviour. That is, Confucianism may not be as reactionary and unsuitable for the modern world as some Chinese radicals have depicted it, but it would not be helpful to see it as superior in every way to modern Western practices. Otherwise, we end up with just a reversed form of stereotyping. For example, when John Biggs tries to resolve the paradox of 'bad' teaching and learning habits with 'good' results among CHC students, he observes that the students in fact have achieved not a superficial but a deep understanding of problems posed, and he comments that 'one of the reliable outcomes of a deep approach is a correct answer' (Biggs, 1996: 45). We must ask: a correct answer to what?

Of course, if the students' sole aim in their work is to achieve good examination results, and they are dedicated towards realising that aim, then they are bound to get skilled in providing 'correct answers' in assessment exercises. But can cultural knowledge have 'correct answers'? The idea that repetition, or rote learning, could lead to deep learning would be appreciated by anyone who plays sport. 'Practice makes perfect' refers not simply to physical excellence. In Chinese culture, for example, calligraphy and painting are said to lead to enlightenment of the mind, as does the practice of martial arts and other repetitive exercises. It is often said that only when a person has mastered the forms and patterns of given tasks, whether in academic disciplines or in martial arts, can a 'deep' understanding of their ultimate goals be achieved. Nonetheless, the point about a 'deep' understanding of these various skills is that, ultimately, there is no 'correct' answer as such. This is not a criticism of Biggs, more a query about paradoxes of cultural knowledge and how to gather that knowledge.

Discarding cultural baggage and gathering meta-cultural sensitivity

Cultural knowledge is so fluid and constantly changing that it is impossible to 'gather' it as if it were a pure and static thing. While CHC, Middle Eastern, Ukrainian or American scholars in Australia or the UK are all international students, the problems they encounter and cultural knowledge they carry are clearly very different. The 'deficit' view of international students is not effective pedagogically because it assumes not only that some cultures are in 'deficit', but that cultural baggage is carried only by students, not teachers. In reality, being the more powerful partner in the teacher–student relationship, the cultural baggage carried by the teachers has a much more dominant effect than that carried by the students. Cultural baggage does not stay stationary, and the teachers must be aware that interactions with students will necessarily impact on both sets of cultures. Unless they are prepared to understand the changes within their own cultures, they are themselves misinformed.

At least for the students, being away from home somewhat frees them of the burden of the cultural baggage. At the same time, being cut adrift from one's culture could also mean a huge sense of insecurity. Cultural baggage can act as a safety net. What is an encumbrance (net that restricts you) can also act as a security (net that stops you from falling). Often, students need to be able to learn how to cut the encumbrances without fear of falling. Teachers may be able to provide the skills to enable students to do so. And to do so involves understanding both host culture and home culture, how these cultures can be both beneficial and harmful. To do so involves 'stepping back' from both cultures and to understand them as systems. That is, to take a meta approach to all cultures. In this chapter, I have used 'culture' as a generalised descriptor. In practice, of course, the student whose parents are professors from Shanghai is going to carry a very different cultural baggage to one whose parents are peasants from a village in Hunan. Meta-cultural sensitivity would need to take into account such individual differences within the 'same culture'.

In any case, it is most important for teachers to help students develop meta-cultural sensitivity. That is, they should be provided with the tools to assess different cultures, particularly the host culture, with understanding and acceptance. It is thus not the gathering of cultural knowledge that is important, but learning how to use the tools. With that skill, all cultures can be appraised and utilised, without having to think that bits and pieces should be valued or condemned. Many students come from rapidly changing cultures and those who succeed in life learn to manage the cultural changes within their own cultures skilfully. In the same way, they will need to learn to manage a new culture/s successfully. This comes from having meta-management skill. In a class with students from very diverse backgrounds, it is a very daunting task for any one individual teacher to claim to have knowledge of the students' very different cultures. In conjunction with the students, however, it may be possible to learn strategies for managing these diverse cultures.

Instead of attempting to 'gather cultural knowledge' as a way to avoid offending the Other/s, working with students to develop the skills and strategies for meta-cultural sensitivity not only helps students appreciate the home and host cultures, but also helps teachers do the same. The development of meta-cultural sensitivity is thus a process of personal growth, through which both the teacher and the student can progressively attain more sophisticated awareness, understanding and acceptance of cultural difference. As a process, it does not represent the acquisition of facts about other cultures, but a changed orientation towards them (Bennett, 1993: 22). Bennett's model identifies the stages ranging from ethnocentrism to ethnorelativism through which individuals move as their cultural understanding increases. In the continuum from distrust to acceptance to ownership, familiarity plays a central role. For example, those who have stayed for a long time in the host country are most likely to show sentiments of fondness and allegiance towards such countries. In countries such as Australia and the UK, where many of the international students are migrants, the 'international' students are in fact 'nationals'.

One of the most exciting things about teaching international students is the possibility for teachers and students to have dynamic interactions. The presence of international students provides an extraordinary learning opportunity for both teachers and students to accept and 'own' each other's culture. In reaching a meta-cultural awareness, the teacher–student partnership is one where the 'partners must be cognizant of their partner's cultural heritage and ... must accord that heritage legitimacy in their dealings with one another' (Smith and Bond, 1999: 287). Of course, such sensitivity does not imply a familiarity with a set of clichéd etiquettes from another culture: the humorous situation in which a Japanese man's extended hand hits the bowing head of an American on greeting each other is one good example of such understanding. In the same way, a Maori student who stares fixedly at a teacher because he has been told that looking at another person in the eye is polite may generate an unexpected, hostile, response. Picking up bits and pieces of another culture is not meta-cultural awareness.

Whether one is teaching international students from Singapore, Italy, Mexico or Ghana, meta-cultural awareness comes with understanding at least two cultures well, including one's own. Knowing the cultures well means the awareness that within all cultures, there are changes, contradictions and ambiguities. Difference occurs not just *between*, but also *within*, cultures. The only constant is that nothing stays the same. Given this, teachers can teach better if they have a deep understanding and an appreciation of the changing nature of their own societies as well as a good knowledge of their students' societies. This sensitivity comes with the ability to be critical of one's own culture while at the same time being empathetic with it. In this way, the teachers can also help students to take a critical look at their native cultures. This is what many of them would want to do in the first place. One of the most precious rewards in cross-border travels is not only the opportunity to learn about other cultures, but the chance to appraise one's own.

References

Ballard, B. and Clanchy, J., 1997, *Teaching International Students: A Brief Guide for Lecturers and Supervisors*. Deakin, ACT: IDP Education Australia.

Bennett, M. J., 1993, 'Towards ethnorelativism: A developmental model of intercultural sensitivity'. In R. M. Paige (ed.) *Education for the Intercultural Experience*. Yarmouth, Maine: Intercultural Press Inc., pp. 21–72.

Biggs, J., 1996, 'Western misperceptions of the Confucian-heritage learning culture'. In Watkins and Biggs (eds) *The Chinese Learner: Cultural, Psychological, and Cultural Influences*. Hong Kong: Comparative Education Research Centre and Melbourne: The Australian Council for Educational Research Ltd, pp. 45–67.

Hofstede, G., 1997, *Cultures and Organizations: Software of the Mind*. New York: McGraw-Hill.

Hofstede, G., 1980, *Culture's Consequences: International Differences in Work-related Values*. Beverly Hills, CA: Sage Publications.

Lee, W.O., 1996, 'The cultural context for Chinese learners: conceptions of learning in the Confucian tradition'. In Watkins and Biggs (eds) *The Chinese Learner: Cultural, Psychological, and Contextual Influences*. Hong Kong: Comparative Education Research Centre and Melbourne: The Australian Council for Educational Research Ltd, pp. 25–41.

Louie, K., 1986, *Inheriting Tradition: Interpretations of the Classical Philosophers in Communist China 1949–1966*. Oxford: Oxford University Press.

Louie, K., 2002, *Theorising Chinese Masculinity: Society and Gender in China*. Cambridge: Cambridge University Press.

Smith, P.B. and Bond, M. H., 1999, *Social Psychology Across Cultures* (2nd edn). Boston: Allyn and Bacon.

The Chinese Culture Connection, 1987, 'Chinese values and the search for culture-free dimensions of culture'. *Journal of Cross-cultural Psychology*, 18 (2), 143–164.

4

Strategies for becoming more explicit

Ms Jude Carroll, Oxford Brookes University

This chapter focuses on practical strategies to help students adapt and succeed in their new surroundings. It stresses the importance of being as explicit as you can be with all students and especially with those coming from different learning and social cultures. Approaches suggested here can be helpful at any time in a student's university career but are especially important at the beginning.

Leask (2004) likens students' arrival at university to learning how to play a new game where success depends on figuring out the new rules, applying them, and 'winning' rewards such as good grades, positive feedback and a sense of confidence and competence as a learner. All students find learning the new university 'game' challenging but international students may be doing so in English, as a second, third or fourth language. British or Australian culture and communication styles may also be unfamiliar and in many cases very different from the home culture (Cortazzi and Jin, 1997). Some international students may not realise the 'rules' have changed and most will start out using behaviours and assumptions that have served them well as learners up to this point. This may mean encountering unpleasant surprises. For example:

- An American student who has always received very high marks does her best at a British university and her first coursework is returned with a mark of 50/100. How could she have earned only half the available marks?
- A Chinese student who has always viewed classrooms as places where you sat, listened and tried to make sense of what was being said by the teacher is asked in an Australian lecture to discuss a point with his neighbour. What is the point of talking to someone who does not know the answer either?
- A Greek student who has previously been rewarded for reading a textbook many times then reproducing its insights in an exam is stunned by a Canadian reading list containing 25 books. How can he cope with that task and three other courses suggesting the same number of books to read?
- A British student with good A levels goes back home after a term's work at a British university and asks, 'Why do my teachers keep asking about referencing my work and giving me bad marks? I got Bs at school.'

Often, when Western teachers are presented with examples like this, they accept that learning is culturally conditioned (see Chapter 2), but awareness of difference can turn to dismay. How can they as teachers familiarise themselves with students' backgrounds when their students come from dozens of different countries? As class sizes rise and workloads grow ever bigger, the chance of spending time with students shrinks. Even if teachers could spend time discussing ideas about learning and teaching, individual students may or may not be sufficiently aware of their own previous learning experiences to provide useful insights and, as Louie reminds us in Chapter 3, it would be dangerous to generalise from the views of one or two students.

I suggest another approach. Teachers can help students best by becoming more knowledgeable about their own academic culture. Once teachers can see their own academic culture as 'systems of belief, expectations and practices about how to perform academically' (Cortazzi and Jin, 1997: 77), they can start to offer explicit help to students who have chosen to learn in that academic culture. Many students will adapt to the Western academic culture without explicit help, of course, by picking up clues and using feedback, observation and implicit messages from teachers to check out their own assumptions. But many others will not. The less insightful and sensitive may not have the time or, in some cases, the confidence and support they need to gradually pick up the rules of the game. Success comes too late or at a very high price in terms of stress, work and worry. Such students will find explicit help vital, though everyone will probably welcome any help that means they can expend less time and energy trying to figure out 'the game' and more time on the content and skills of the programme itself.

Another significant benefit from becoming aware of one's own academic culture is that it allows more flexibility and choice. Once the system becomes visible, it is possible to move from assuming that international students will adopt Western academic values, to being clear about what can and cannot be adapted, so that it is possible for students to succeed as learners in the new academic culture.

It follows, then, that being explicit with students starts with being self-aware about one's own academic culture, or what Louie (Chapter 3) calls becoming 'meta-aware'.

Becoming self-aware

Some teachers (and indeed, some people) do not see themselves as carriers of culture, assigning that role only to their incoming students. They take for granted the correct way to behave in seminars, the structure of an essay, the appropriate way for students to interact with teachers, and so on. If teachers have only worked within one academic culture with others who share similar beliefs, such things do not seem to involve culture at all; they seem logical, normal and obvious. Only when one encounters someone with different views do one's own assumptions become obvious, sometimes acutely so. A colleague tells the story of how she never thought about buying her meat until she travelled in Sudan and met women who were shocked that she frequented a butcher's shop. My colleague commented, 'I never thought of myself as serving dead meat until I saw their reaction'.

Some tutors and lecturers have experienced stepping outside the normal when they worked in other cultures or tried to be successful students in others' learning cultures. Some have tried to do themselves justice in a new language. The majority of Western academics, however, only encounter opportunities for making their teaching and learning assumptions visible through interacting with students and colleagues arriving from other social and learning cultures. This is not always a welcome opportunity.

We tend to react negatively when the culturally unexpected occurs (though, of course, pleasant surprises do happen). For example, people from the UK who travel to China often talk about how Chinese people deal with spitting. The experience can simply trigger disgust or it can make the UK traveller aware (perhaps for the first time) of his own, different spitting conventions through the surprise of encountering others with different views. I certainly was unaware of the strategies I internalised when growing up in the US for making a request, but I did notice (probably because the two communication styles were reasonably similar) how others reacted to what had previously been appropriate behaviour when I tried using it in Britain. British people, I decided, do ask others to do things but they ask differently. British reaction allowed me to both articulate my previous beliefs and begin to sketch out my assumptions about how to be acceptable (and hopefully, accepted) in the UK.

Many of the encounters between teachers and students are like the spitting, asking and butchering examples, i.e. situated at the more general level of cultural assumptions about communication styles, ways of negotiating, dealing with conflict, planning time, and so on. However, this chapter seeks to narrow the focus to specific beliefs and assumptions linked to learning.

Louie in Chapter 3 talks of 'stepping back' from cultures and trying to understand them as systems, noting 'This sensitivity comes with the ability to be critical of one's own culture while at the same time being empathetic with it' (p.24). Often, teachers talk about difference only as disappointment, rather than the sensitivity and empathy that Louie suggests. It is possible to elicit positive aspects of the differences international students bring as learners. Teachers mention international students' wider experience. Teachers often appreciate students' diligent work habits and respect for teachers and for learning. It is much more common, however, for hard-pressed lecturers to see international students as the negative expression of their own cultural values ('they never speak', 'they plagiarise', 'they want too much support', 'they take too much of my time'). Of course, some students (both international and domestic) are over-demanding. Some do cheat. Some withdraw into silence. But before blaming the student, it might help to first consider whether students are using old rules for a new game. Blame then becomes thinking about how to help students adapt and learn new skills to fit them for the new tasks they will meet in Western universities.

Noticing and using surprises

When British lecturers are asked, 'What do international students do that you don't expect from home students? Are there any unexpected behaviours?' lecturers mention behaviours such as:

- giving presents
- answering all my questions with 'yes'
- calling me Dr X even when I have said 'call me John'
- complaining about wasting time on seminars rather than me teaching
- handing in 4,000 words for an essay with a 2,500 limit
- writing very personal coursework with the main point on page 3 and lots of unnecessary background
- repeating verbatim my lecture notes in the coursework
- coming into my office after I have given the marks to argue loudly that I should give them higher marks – several times
- remaining silent in seminars even when I ask a direct question
- coming up after the lecture for a 1:1 discussion and seeming to expect me to stay for as long as it takes even though I said 'Any questions?' in the lecture
- deferring to my opinion even when a preference would be appropriate (e.g. Me: 'Which essay will you do as coursework?' Student: 'Please, you say')
- talking loudly in lectures

You can probably add your own experiences to the list, even if you have been teaching international students for long enough so that such events no longer actually surprise you. In each of the examples cited, it is likely that the student is using different 'rules' from their teachers. Often, this mismatch is interpreted negatively, so giving presents may be viewed as bribery, writing 1,500 extra words is seen as disorganised, arguing for a better mark is interpreted as pushy, talking in lectures is labelled as rude, and so on. A British or Australian teacher probably automatically assumes the behaviour has the same (unwelcome) meaning in an international student as it would have in a home student who acted that way.

Meta-awareness means moving beyond spontaneous first reactions to identify what you were assuming would happen – looking for the invisible normal 'rule'. One group of British teachers generated a list of 'surprises' then came up with these academic cultural 'rules':

- *Presents:* Presents are OK but only after the mark has been assigned. The present should be small and preferably disposable/edible. It is more common to send a thank-you card or note.
- *Word length:* Not negotiable and designates a maximum. Staying within the limit is evidence of self-organisation. More words are not a sign of hard work.
- *Seeking changes in marks:* This can be done but only if teachers disagree with each other, not in response to students' pressing for change.

- *Teachers' names:* Use the name suggested. Many teachers expect first names except in formal or public situations. Calling by first names does not signify friendship or imply an equal status between student and teacher.
- *Speaking in seminars:* British tutors tend to like students' active involvement and expect them to spell things out even if the teacher already knows it. Speaking is valued more than listening though speaking after listening and thinking is best. Students clarify their thoughts by speaking. Getting it wrong helps students see where they need to think differently.
- *Reproducing verbatim notes:* Modifying texts shows the student has understood. Students' work should be individually created. Tutor notes may be used as a resource for drawing personal conclusions but when used, must be cited.
- *Putting the main point of an essay on the third page:* Western writing is generally deductive, i.e. the main point comes first followed by background information and supporting arguments. Building rapport with the reader and providing background at the beginning is 'waffling'.

Not everyone in the group agreed about every point in this example but they did agree that a student behaving in the ways they described would progress through their classroom without notice or comment. A more interesting discussion centred on whether they as teachers had the right to ask for such changes and how they would cope should the student be unwilling or unable to adopt these new behaviours. I will return to this point at the end of the chapter, turning first to how teachers can help students learn Western academic cultural 'rules' and beliefs.

Being explicit

Once you become aware of cultural difference, you can re-interpret the student's previously negatively viewed behaviour, using a well-established technique sometimes called *cultural repair*. For example, 'repaired' thinking might be, 'This present is probably not a bribe; it probably arises from different ideas about gift giving.' Often, the best response is to keep 'repaired' reactions to yourself. However, there are times when it is helpful to give the other person information about your own academic culture because it is an important matter or because it would help the student to be more successful. Although studies have shown that students welcome specific guidance (Cortazzi and Jin, 1997), teachers often shy away from giving the student specific information about Western academic culture, perhaps because they are concerned about appearing patronising or of seeming to criticise students' previous experiences. A few lecturers hold back from being explicit because they believe learning to fit in is part of a student's task just as learning to figure out what an essay question means is part of the assessment. Some find being explicit too much effort due to frantic schedules, demanding workloads or even personal inclination.

Whatever the cause, a teacher's reluctance to explain may leave the student no option but to get it wrong, notice the consequences and decide what would have been more appropriate – a painful and time-consuming learning strategy. It does not follow, however, that repeatedly and meticulously explaining everything to a student is either possible or helpful. Too much explicitness becomes overwhelming and stifles the student's own sensitivity and curiosity. Explanations, even explicit ones, contain significant amounts of tacit and implied knowledge so teachers need to select their opportunities and students will need time and experience and practice to make sense of any guidance.

Even statements that seem explicit, such as, 'Ensure your essay draws on a wide range of sources to support your argument' may still leave the student baffled as it includes tacit and shared knowledge. For example, what might constitute 'a wide range' or even what is an essay? The person giving advice might assume that writing is based on posing and defending a particular point of view. All these things might be new and perhaps strange ideas for many international students. By building in practice, feedback, a chance to see examples of good and poor work, and opportunities to try out new skills, students can turn this explicit advice into something that makes sense.

Given time and sensitive feedback, students can develop these skills themselves. Wisker (2003) talks about helping students to 'hang in there and keep going' through those difficult early months. A teacher's skill lies in knowing when to be explicit, how much to explain and what to be explicit about. If you are unsure where to start, four areas seem to hold the most difficulty for students new to the Western academic game. You could especially try to be explicit about:

- teaching methods;
- assessment;
- teacher–student relationships; and
- academic writing.

Being explicit about teaching methods

Many international students (and probably most home students) have spent years in systems where:

- teachers tell and students listen;
- students tutor each other outside class and co-operate in completing work, often copying each others' answers;
- tasks are highly structured and teacher-directed;
- there is lots of homework, tested orally in class;
- a high value is placed on knowing information and accessing it quickly but low value is placed on using information or evaluating it; and
- personal diligence (expressed as time on homework) is the norm.

What are the Western characteristics, expectations and assumptions that students moving from those types of learning environments might find strange or alarming?

How would reactions and behaviours such students might show in their new setting give you a clue as to how your own academic culture is different?

Students new to Western universities usually welcome explanations as to the purpose of lectures, or the benefits of discussion-based learning, or the link between out-of-class tasks (rather than structured homework) and independent learning. Students new to seminars would find it useful to be aware of what you value and/or expect. Do you generally prefer talking over listening, dialogue over reflection, and creativity over consensus and pragmatic solutions? Can you tell students how you expect them to behave in ways that will make sense to someone who does not share those views?

By observing your students and discussing their experiences, other issues may emerge. What lies behind the Western use of group learning? How are group tasks assessed? How is a student expected to structure his or her time in your university? What is supposed to happen in the library? You can doubtless generate many more questions.

Once you know what your assumptions are, it will help your students if you share with them some of those assumptions as explicitly as you can.

Being explicit about assessment

Often, it is not until the end of the first term when students submit an assignment and do badly that they realise their ideas about assessment may not match your own. Again, to know what to be explicit about, you need to look for what your international students struggle with then offer information. Spell out dates, times and deadlines; it generally takes international students much longer to accomplish tasks compared to domestic students. Students being assessed usually welcome explicit instructions on:

- the length of submissions (and the fact that longer is not better);
- the format (with explanations of what a report, poster, essay or précis might be and possibly a chance to try out new formats such as oral presentations and viva voces);
- what the assessment criteria mean and how they are applied;
- what is being assessed (especially the percentage of the mark allocated to English language proficiency); and
- which aspects of the assessment brief are compulsory and which are guidance or suggestions.

Because assessment is so central to academic culture, it helps to ensure information is conveyed in writing as well as through discussion, explanation or example.

Being explicit about assessment also includes thinking about feedback. Explicit, sensitive feedback acknowledges students' efforts and guides them to a more acceptable performance. Feedback that concentrates on what students have not done ('confusing argument', 'no links') or that implies rather than states what is required ('Is this your own words?', 'What about the Hastings report?') is not helpful. It assumes the student knows the preferred behaviour, can decode the question, and could do what you suggest if they wished. This kind of feedback is rather like telling someone who is unskilled at Indian cookery how not to make a curry by writing 'coconut?'. Explicit feedback describes positive behaviour ('Put the main idea first then provide examples of how the idea would work in practice' or 'Tell the reader when you move from describing the method to discussing whether it is a good method or not' or 'If you are using someone else's words, you must enclose their words in quotation marks to show they are not your own words' or 'You should have referred to the Hastings report because it ...').

As a significant number of students often make similar mistakes based on similar assumptions, it is possible to assemble statement banks to streamline the task. Confine your comments to key points or essential information, especially in the early days, so as not to overwhelm students. Peer and self-assessment methods, perhaps in a workshop setting, can be useful ways to explore and clarify assumptions (Price *et al.*, 2001) if you and the students are clear as to the purpose of the workshop.

Being explicit about teacher–student relationships

Students' previous experience may have included:

- teachers as experts and authorities, providing answers;
- teachers acting as parental figures, guiding and being involved with the student as a person;
- teachers knowing students' problems and guiding them to solutions;
- teachers giving clear instructions on what students must do; and
- teachers being generally available to students out of class.

Students may behave as if these relationships will continue in the Western university and may welcome sensitive guidance on what they can and cannot expect from you as a teacher. When can they see you? What issues are appropriate to bring to a tutorial? If (as is usually the case in Western universities) students must ask for help if there are problems, how might the student learn to express their needs to teachers rather than expecting others to notice? If you see teaching as facilitating or organising students' learning rather than as providing answers, how can you help students see you in this new light?

A word about empathy

Differences are often deeply held beliefs rather than superficial matters of learning new table manners or ways of greeting others. Adapting and accepting new ways will be hard for all students and may even be impossible for some. Teachers may need to be patient, sensitive and adaptable themselves as well as explicit with students attempting to adjust to Western academic culture. The more teachers are aware of their own culture, the more likely they are to be able to help international students adjust and thrive in the new academic culture they have (sometimes unwittingly) chosen to experience. Self-awareness also lets teachers be more flexible about what can be modified to allow students to show the same learning to the same standard but doing so differently. Once teachers are clear about which core values, beliefs and behaviours are essential elements of a Western university qualification, they know what can and cannot be adapted, what can and cannot be made optional, and what must be demonstrated by students wanting that qualification. Your explicit guidance will help all students progress towards those goals.

References

Cortazzi, M. and Jin, L. (1997). 'Communication for learning across cultures'. In D. McNamara and R. Harris (eds) *Overseas Students in Higher Education: Issues on Teaching and Learning*. London: Routledge.

Leask, B. (2004). 'Plagiarism and cultural diversity: responsibilities, accountabilities and pedagogy'. *Plagiarism: Prevention, Practice and Policy Conference*, Northumbria University, 28–30 June 2004.

Price, M., O'Donovan, B. and Rust, C. (2001). 'Strategies to develop students' understanding of assessment criteria and processes'. In C. Rust (ed.) *Improving Student Learning – 8: Improving Student Learning Strategically*. Oxford: Oxford Centre for Staff and Learning Development.

Wisker, G. (2003). 'Hanging on in there, a long way from home', *Educational Development*, 4: 4, 21.

5

'Lightening the load'

Teaching in English, learning in English

Ms Jude Carroll, Oxford Brookes University

Much of this book addresses ways that students adapt to and learn in different academic cultures. This chapter focuses on the fact that a significant proportion of international students' adaptation and learning in Western universities occurs in a new and perhaps unfamiliar language, English. In my own university, the 2003 statistics showed 40 countries had 'sent' 10 or more students. Looking down the list:

*   25 (62 per cent) were countries where students probably neither used English at home nor studied in the medium before enrolling in UK tertiary education
*   11 (27 per cent) were countries where students may have had some or all of their secondary schooling from teachers using English, either as a first or (more probably) as second language.

In the UK as a whole, the British Council listed the 20 countries that sent the most students (a total of 131,520) along with the number from each country. A quick look at the list showed:

*   65,790 (50 per cent) being from countries where English is unlikely to be the language of instruction
*   47,680 (36 per cent) from countries where English is probably the language of instruction but is not the students' or teachers' first language
*   14,365 (11 per cent) who are probably native English speakers, taught by native English speakers.

Source: British Council, 2003/4

Second-language lecturers in the Caribbean, India, Sri Lanka, Ghana, or the Lebanon may use a variation of English unlike the one students encounter in a Western university. Even native speakers find surprising and sometimes discomforting differences when they move from one English-speaking country to another though this is a minor matter compared to those arriving with an untested and probably imperfect grasp of English.

Are teaching difficulties language-based?

Whenever lecturers and tutors discuss the issues in teaching international students, they usually place more emphasis on language competency than on any other issue (Robertson *et al.*, 2000). Research demonstrates that English as a Foreign Language (EFL, referred to as English as a Second Language students in Australia) students with low language competency can survive and even thrive if the environment is supportive and inclusive (Asmar, 1999). However, teachers and students readily describe difficulties that they attribute to students' lack of language skills.

The fact that EFL students find study in Western universities difficult is hardly surprising as anyone will attest who has tried to master and use another language to go beyond everyday activities such as ordering a meal, chatting about one's family or arguing with a garage mechanic. A few weeks of pre-sessional language teaching can be of great benefit but an EFL student may take many months to gain language competence. Most take longer still to feel confident in expressing abstract ideas or using complex skills such as those described in Chapters 6 and 7. It takes skill, practice and time to begin to do oneself justice in another language and EFL students doing a top-up final year in a three-year degree or enrolled on a one-year Masters may never have that opportunity. For these groups, mastering English will probably remain among the most difficult aspects of their study. All students, even those who stay long enough to get to grips with English, will find the early weeks and months problematic. This chapter suggests practical ways to help students make the transition to studying *in English*. Effort to do so is justified because if teachers lighten students' language load, students can free up thinking space for the other things they need to be successful.

Minimum proficiency requirements

Most universities have a range of ways to support non-native English speakers, usually starting with requiring a minimal language proficiency to secure admission. A few have no such requirement, presumably with the short-term aim of encouraging enrolment. The longer-term result of such a policy is almost completely negative: failing international students, angry home students, negative teaching experiences and sometimes, media exposure of low-quality institutional provision. By requiring a realistic and sustainable minimal language competence for admission, an institution is making a key step towards supporting all students' learning. It may take persuasion, persistence and statistics to convince recruiters and marketing people that admitting more students is not preferable to admitting more skilful students. Many will need convincing that if they say 'no' to some, there will be others.

Ideally, minimum proficiency requirements will be tailored to the demands of specific programmes with higher entrance scores in programmes where English itself is an integral part of the learning outcomes. Adjusting the threshold will address some concerns teachers regularly express about teaching non-native

English speakers but is unlikely to preclude teachers saying disparaging things about their students. In unguarded moments or when rendered impatient by increasing demands, you will probably hear 'What are they doing here if they can't speak English?' or 'These students passed the language test but don't understand a word'. Some of teachers' frustration arises from not understanding what the tests can and cannot show and what the scoring means. One test, the International English Language Testing Scheme or IELTS, is the most widely used in the UK and Australia (though worldwide, it is more likely to find students admitted on the basis of the Test of English as a Foreign Language, known as TOEFL scores). IELTS assesses a student's ability to read, write, speak and understand English by asking them to do tasks. However, the tasks are short (the largest writing task is a personal opinion essay of 250 words) and dissimilar to those students will encounter in an English-speaking university. The tests, therefore, can give some indication of the student's overall language skill but offer little guidance as to abilities suitable for an academic environment.

A second source of misunderstanding of students' language competence arises from the mixture of abilities that are being tested. In the IELTS, for example, students are scored for reading, writing, listening and speaking (usually with 4 as a minimum and 9 as maximum) but each of these bands is very broad, containing a wide variation in competence. Two students with scores of 5.0 may have very different abilities in reading. The final score is derived from averaging the four sub-scores resulting in a single score that further masks these variations. Thus, a student with an IELTS score of 6.0 could have scored low on speaking and listening/understanding and high on reading and writing. This variation is one reason why it is always a good idea, if a teacher encounters a student who appears not to understand, to use a different form of words or another means of communication by, for example, abandoning speaking and trying writing it down and vice versa. (This point will be touched on again when considering ways of conveying information.) Because variation in competency may cause difficulties in programmes that rely on one sort of language skill, many institutions stipulate a minimum overall IELTS score and a particular aspect minimum ('a 6.5 with nothing below 6').

The limitations of current language testing go beyond interpreting the results and are probably here to stay. An academic test that actually tested academic language proficiency and set realistic tasks yet remained practical in terms of time, delivery methods and scoring is probably beyond any examination organisation's ability. A minimum score can, however, show how much pre-sessional help a student will need and provide guidance as to the extra support that will be appropriate in the early months of the programme. Many institutions recognise these limits and retest students on arrival to confirm scores and seek more guidance on their abilities. This permits checking English competence in a discipline-specific context. Some use early diagnostic exercises to guide students to additional support by English language specialists. Where extra help is available, students generally welcome it although many find it difficult to make time for additional work in their already pressured schedules. Another difficulty with add-on English support arises when students seek to transfer generic help into skills relevant to their discipline-based work. One English Language lecturer who has supported UK-based EFL students for many years comments:

> The best scenario is when students have the relevant skills in place prior to the start of their academic programme so they only need to adjust to the discourse and content of their discipline ... where everyone – prospective students, educational agents, and university admission staff – recognise the value of pre-sessional courses. This is rare.

Students' perceptions of their language skills

Before turning to specific suggestions for those who teach EFL speakers, it is worth mentioning that previous comments about teachers' misunderstanding of entrance scores can apply equally to students. Before they travel to a Western university, many students assume their training in English as expressed in their test score will give them enough language capacity to cope. They consider themselves English speakers. On arrival, they suddenly meet real English rather than the often careful and sedately paced variety they have previously experienced in classrooms or from teachers who are using English as a second language. This change, plus a local accent, discipline-specific vocabulary, and the sheer hard work of using English all day, can severely dent students' previous confidence. Everyone's language proficiency varies depending on the situation and the early days of learning in a new academic culture are amongst the most stressful many students will ever encounter. An extensive literature on so-called 'culture shock' in those early weeks and months documents how confidence dips and students struggle with even the most ordinary tasks, including language matters. It is not uncommon for students to swing from inaccurate confidence that they *can* speak English to an equally inaccurate conclusion that they cannot.

The same crisis of confidence can be seen in students who leave specially tailored foundation programmes in their chosen university where they have been taught by EFL specialists and where the majority of students are also international students. The University of Northumbria in the UK interviewed students attending a one-year pre-university foundation programme and found 15 per cent thought teachers spoke too quickly. Six months into their university programmes (and with the benefit of that much more practice), the same students said 30 per cent of teachers were 'too fast' (Smailes and Gannon-Leary, 2004). For these students, the 'real world' proved to be a very testing place where the language challenges described in the previous paragraph were compounded by subject teachers' not doing what EFL specialists do almost as second nature. The students in EFL courses may not have noted the benefits of teachers who, as a matter of course and arising from the nature of their teaching, repeated information, invited students to speak or waited for answers, until they had transferred to mainstream courses where this did not happen. An even more dramatic shift was found for students' writing, where researchers describe the students as 'plummeting' from 63 per cent who felt they could clearly express ideas in writing to 31 per cent six months later in their undergraduate course (Smailes and Gannon-Leary, 2004, p. 10).

Specialist units to support English

Teachers can sometimes call on others to help their students who are new to study in English. If you teach in an institution that provides extra language support for students, you will maximise this resource by making clear to students that attendance is an integral part of their course and by improving your links with EFL specialists. You could find out exactly what kind of support is on offer and what is not generally available. For example, few specialist units provide a proofreading service but many will help a student learn to structure coursework to fit lecturers' expectations. Better liaison would also allow both sides – subject lecturer and English language support lecturer – to share information about what is expected, how assessment criteria are applied for home and international students, and the areas where international students have particular difficulties such as decoding impenetrable assignment briefs or understanding scribbled comments in the margins of their returned work.

Many subject teachers would like specialist units to support all students' language needs so they, the subject teachers, can focus solely on content knowledge. However, even with reasonably high entrance requirements in place and reasonably comprehensive generic support on offer (a minority of cases, it must be said), teachers themselves remain the most significant facilitator of students' adjustments to studying in English. Nothing can help better than teachers' actions and no one can help more frequently than the teachers those students encounter day in and day out. All students, native speakers and EFL speakers, will need a teacher's help to learn the language of their discipline. The rest of this chapter outlines ways this could be done, leaving the aspects related to writing to Chapter 7 and other academic skills to Chapter 6.

'Early English' strategies

Suggesting that higher education lecturers pay attention to how they use English, especially at the start of a programme, can be problematic. Many teachers enjoy creating complex, often entertaining, presentations for their students. They relish choosing just the right word to make a point, adopting a metaphor and throwing in a joke to keep students alert. After years of using what others call jargon, academics view the language of their discipline as straightforward and often, as the most accurate and efficient way to explain ideas. Students, especially international students, do not necessarily see all these as positive, although later on everyone can begin to enjoy these aspects and behave much less self-consciously.

If you want to free up your students' thinking time so they can spend less time decoding what you say and more time engaging with your ideas, a good place to start is by using what has been called 'Plain English'. Plain English uses common words ('bleed' instead of 'haemorrhage', 'help' instead of 'facilitate', 'house' instead of 'dwelling'). Speakers are encouraged to avoid introductory phrases and state things in chronological order. Instead of saying, 'Before drafting an ad to recruit a new member of staff, it is important to consider the current job description …', Plain English speakers say, 'First, think about the current job description. Does anything need to change? If it does need to change, make the changes and then use the new job description to write an advertisement …'. This kind of English encourages short sentences, favours the active voice over the passive and avoids unnecessary words (i.e. not, 'if, on the other hand, you find yourself in a position to be able to' but rather, 'If you can …'). Sentences that have a subject–verb–object format are easier to follow, especially if they mirror the order in which things should be done (although resorting to Tarzan talk as in 'You go Library' will offend even the most rudimentary English speaker). The same Plain English is equally important in written documents such as handbooks and course guides.

It does not help EFL students to simply speak more slowly (or loudly!) and doing so may frustrate the EFL student, the rest of the class and the speaker him- or herself. Instead, finishing words by saying the last syllable or consonant before moving to the next word usually slows you down without distorting stress patterns or intonation. It may be impossible to sustain the effort so perhaps this tactic is best left for important messages only. Normally, talking more slowly is less useful than pausing after introducing a new idea. A brief pause will allow those who must both translate and consider an idea the time they need to do both things; those who do not need to translate usually welcome the chance to think about a new idea, too. Another useful tactic is to use careful, sensitive repetition of exactly the same phrase when making an important point or when speaking with a student showing signs of having misunderstood. Verbatim repetition can stress the information's importance to all students and give EFL students another chance to translate the message because, although a paraphrase may help native English speakers, it puts EFL students back to square one.

You may or may not have noticed that the last paragraph finished with a metaphor, i.e. one that compared understanding English to playing a game like hopscotch. Metaphors and analogies are forms of verbal gymnastics that fox students and can scupper their chances of understanding what you mean. Sometimes, as in the last sentence, metaphors and analogies are obvious but usually, speakers are unaware that their mentions of landslide victories, parent companies or brownfield sites include these forms of speech. Metaphors not only confuse novice speakers, they also rely on significant amounts of cultural knowledge. If you do use them, research has shown that people remember them better when told the origin rather than the meaning. For example, a colleague on a recruiting tour of Southeast Asia heard locals referring to one university's agents as 'wild chickens'. Explaining that this meant they were not selective was less helpful than being told that wild chickens eat everything in the forest. Since there is not time to explain in many cases, avoiding metaphors may be best, though this usually requires a combination of self-policing (a metaphor?) and encouraging students to alert you when you have used one. The latter suggestion will be considered in the next section after a final word about jokes.

It is probably useful when teaching a diverse student group, especially one you do not know well, to avoid jokes. This seems harsh. Laughing together can lighten the mood, encourage friendly relationships, and foster a sense of sharing. But jokes are risky, too. They depend on often intimate cultural knowledge and assume a shared sense of what is funny. I well remember watching a British comedy by Monty Python in a Midwestern US cinema and being the only person in the theatre who was laughing. Often, jokes build solidarity by creating exclusion, an 'us and them'. Few will feel included when they cannot understand the reference or do not find the remark funny, even if it is not designed to exclude them. In time, as you begin to know your students and they know you, it may be possible to enjoy and share a laugh. Certainly, the world would be a duller place without humour but early on, a useful rule might be: when in doubt, don't.

Providing classroom-based ad hoc language support

Early in the programme, it will help all students to overtly use and define discipline-specific vocabulary. One way to do this is to hand out a glossary and ask students to contribute new words, building the resource year on year. It is likely to be a more dynamic and collaborative tool if you collect unfamiliar disciplinary vocabulary whilst teaching by, for example, setting up a flip chart and asking students to alert you to a new word as you or others use it. Simply jotting the word down usually does not interfere with the flow of the ideas and content of the session and if the same list is posted week after week, a bespoke resource will emerge. A colleague has added a twist to this idea by handing out yellow cards to students who need only lift one to alert her to the use of a new word without drawing undue attention during a session. Students said they liked this approach because they did not want to interrupt the teacher and they could learn vocabulary in context.

Most students, but especially non-native speakers, also welcome handouts and pre-printed notes. Many will have never experienced taking notes or making their own record of a session so they will be struggling with the process itself as well as the English language component. Indeed, one reason that international students are frequently characterised as passive and silent in lectures is that they are using every ounce of their energies in trying to keep up with what is happening. Gapped notes (that is, where some of the information such as complex diagrams or significant headings are provided with gaps left for the student to add further information) are a useful way to help students move from unskilled novice to becoming able to make useful records of lectures and tutorials. You could also consider either recording sessions yourself, perhaps making the result available on the intranet or in the library, or suggest students make their own recording. An advantage of audiotapes is that they give students several chances to extract meaning; however, the significant disadvantage is that they take a large amount of students' time. The danger is that they might focus too much on what has happened, leaving insufficient time for planning and being prepared for the next session(s).

Building on the last point about preparation time, teachers can help all students, and especially their international students, by providing adequate warning and building in preparation tasks. For example, when lecturing, a glossary of terms provided the week before, or a list of the key topics, or a suggestion of a relatively small amount of introductory reading will encourage students to come ready to listen and make sense of the lecture. This kind of pre-warning goes well beyond telling them the title. In the same way, building in warnings in seminars will help all students to participate. This involves saying things like, 'In five minutes, I will ask for your views on xxx. Can you jot down a few ideas about how you would answer this question.' Or 'I want to hear your ideas about the influence of xxx on yyy. Can you turn to your neighbour and list two or three ways the two are connected then I will call on two or three partners to tell me what they came up with.' Pairing can provide opportunities for two speakers of the same language to exchange ideas and concepts and to rehearse their ideas before sharing them in English (if you encourage this behaviour). Or pairing can allow two students with different languages to use English to clarify ideas and possibly vocabulary with a classmate before attempting the same in a large group. All students would find the latter helpful.

Another way to encourage all students, including EFL students, to speak is to ask the same question to a series of students, calling on the international students in the third or fourth 'slot' (note: this works best with an open question with many possible answers). Perhaps the simplest suggestion is to increase the time you wait for students to answer. Apparently, the average time a teacher waits for students to answer is less than five seconds before asking a supplementary question. Doubling the wait to ten seconds might make a real difference to those composing an answer. All the seminar management strategies that hold back the eager responders who often prevent others from having their say and who are not necessarily your most thoughtful contributors will help students, including EFL students, have their say.

References

Asmar, C. (1999). 'Scholarship, experience or both?: A developer's approach to cross-cultural teaching'. *International Journal for Academic Development*, 4 (1), 18–27.

British Council (2003/2004) www.britcoun.org/ecs/reports/review_of_the_year/index.htm#year2003-2004

Robertson, M., Line, M., Jones, S. and Thomas, S. (2000). 'International students, learning environments and perceptions: A case study using the Delphi technique'. *Higher Education Research and Development*, 19 (1), 89–102.

Smailes, J. and Gannon-Leary, P. (2004). 'International students – from ELAN to NBS'. *RECAP Series: Researching the Challenges in Academic Practices*, University of Northumbria at Newcastle.

Part II

Methodologies and pedagogies

6

Building intercultural competencies

Implications for academic skills development

Dr Patricia McLean, University of Melbourne
Ms Laurie Ransom, University of Melbourne

The transition to university is a new experience for each student, with all students expected to develop new ways of thinking, learning and communicating. Many students (although this is less common in Australia) will also be adjusting to living away from home for the first time and will be absent from familiar support networks. The vocabulary of a new discipline will be as foreign to local students as it is to international students, and accepted Western academic styles of communication may be equally unfamiliar to many local students from educationally disadvantaged backgrounds. The diversity evident in classrooms worldwide includes difference based on factors such as age, gender, religion, disability, educational background and class. It is an all-inclusive mixture of differences and similarities along a given dimension and contributes substantially to the complexity of individual learning styles and background experiences evident in any classroom. For students, developing the intercultural expertise to successfully navigate a new culture is a prerequisite of university success; it will also be a prerequisite for success in increasingly transnational workplaces.

With increasing commodification of the higher education sector, concern about the language and academic skills of international students is of political and economic as well as pedagogical concern. What is not always acknowledged is the culturally imperialistic way in which concerns about language and academic skills of international students are often considered. In most universities, it is expected that international students perform in and are assessed against the conventions of the host country's educational values and practices; it is further assumed that students will know and understand these. This deficit approach (Smart *et al.*, 1998) like many of the early culture shock theorists,[1] implies that any 'problem' is the student's, that it is the role of academics and language support staff to 'correct' the problem and that it is the student's responsibility to 'adjust'.

Lawrence (2001) places part of the responsibility for this 'problem' on lack of understanding of an increasingly diverse student population and the range of educational backgrounds and experiences that they bring. Lawrence suggests many academics are still teaching to the 'elite' rather than the 'actual'; that they limit themselves to 'pure' teaching rather than a 'value-added' style of teaching which supports students in the learning process (Lawrence, 2001, p. 4).

This chapter explores the cultural learning students bring with them, how it can influence their access to learning, and implications for academic skills development. A key focus will be the analysis of cultural issues underlying tertiary academic skills and suggestions for pedagogical strategies to 'value-add' in terms of developing the intercultural competencies necessary for success in higher education and eventually, for employment in a global market place.

Towards an inclusive classroom

Australian authors Mullins, Quintrell and Hancock (1995) suggest that international students experience three to four times more difficulties than their local counterparts in writing assignments and participating in tutorials; they mention twice as often their fear of failure, nervousness and trouble understanding lecturers. On 'quality of teaching' surveys, students cite the following areas as needing improvement: quality of the teacher explanations, clarity of course aims and objectives, and helpfulness of staff outside of teaching hours (Baldwin, Jones and Prince, 1998).

Best practice in teaching in a diverse classroom means taking the time to explore what skills and experiences our international cohort brings, and what expectations they have of teachers. Althen (as cited in Bennett, 1988, pp. 132–34) suggests the following for facilitating intercultural communication in the classroom: tolerance of ambiguity, respect for difference, curiosity, cognitive complexity, humour and humility, and empathy. Inclusive communication involves each of these attributes and involves not only developing a greater understanding of cultural differences but the importance of developing a larger repertoire of skills and strategies to accommodate the diverse cultural frameworks of our students.

Building intercultural expertise in classroom interactions

Approaches to learning are inherently culturally bound with educational values, behaviours and skills taught from birth and honed through the formative years without much conscious awareness. Students, therefore, are often unaware that their academic skills and behaviours may not match those expected by their teachers, and vice versa. For both students and staff, there are two concurrent pathways to developing intercultural competencies:

1   To become more aware of your own cultural 'pre-programming', to understand the assumptions that underpin your own thinking, learning, writing and communication styles – all the expectations, interpretations, and understandings which are so much part of your consciousness that they are often overlooked. This issue is addressed in more detail in Chapter 4.
2   To learn about the cultural encoding of others. This goes beyond linguistic, racial or ethnic difference to include the way we think, teach and learn.

Our life experiences are also shaped by such things as age, gender, work experience and academic discipline.

For most university teachers, the academic culture inherent in their discipline seems obvious and expectations are rarely made explicit. In practice, however, we have learned how to behave in tutorials and lectures, expectations of the postgraduate–supervisor relationship, out-of-class etiquette, and attitudes to cheating and intellectual property. These are all potential causes of misunderstanding and miscommunication when we encounter those who have learned about these matters differently. Most teachers can tell stories of these kinds of misunderstandings. Here are some of ours:

> A group of American students on exchange to our Australian university were appalled by what they perceived as lack of respect from Aussie students who put their feet on the seats and interrupted the lecturer constantly.

> An Australian lecturer was annoyed because the Chinese students in his tutorial would always wait to the end of the lecture before coming up to ask questions. 'Not only does it mean I'm always kept behind for at least half an hour, but some of the questions are really terrific and it's such a wasted learning opportunity for the others.'

> When her lecturer expressed concern about the high level of plagiarism in a Thai student's last essay, the young woman was horrified … 'but I *did* pay for the book!'

> An American teacher in China was upset when her supervisor advised her of a student's complaint about his mark on a recent assessment task. To her, this was a reprimand, and she was both shocked and angry to think that her student had gone 'above' her to complain. To her student, this was the most respectful way to indicate his unhappiness and request reconsideration of the mark.

> An Australian lecturer who had spent some considerable time developing what he called a 'cheat sheet' that he thought would help his students was bemused when the Asian students in his class refused to use it in exams.

> The young supervisor of a Korean PhD student was embarrassed by the expensive gift he received from his student when she returned from the summer vacation and assumed she was trying to 'buy' his goodwill.

Hofstede (1986) describes in detail how an individual's cognitive development is determined by the demands of their environment and how we master skills that are valued and repeated often. For example, the ability to recognise pattern is generally undervalued by Western academics but critical to learning Chinese which has over

200 radicals and thousands of stems, only mastered after repeated practice and so called 'rote' learning (Redding, 1980 as cited in Hofstede, 1986). An Australian student will just as easily anger his professor in Korea by openly questioning the content of the lectures as will a Chinese student exasperate her Australian post-graduate supervisor by reproducing texts.

Working with students whose cognitive competencies differ from those of the teacher requires a different didactic approach. Being aware of these differences and applying a systematic approach to teaching the metacognitive skills necessary for success in the new academic culture are integral to value-added teaching. Accurate student assessment followed by appropriate interventions and feedback requires a careful consideration of each particular behaviour in the cultural context in which that behaviour was learned.

Teaching styles across cultures

Hofstede (1986) in his seminal research describes four dimensions of cultural difference: individualism/collectivism, power distance, masculinity/femininity and uncertainty avoidance, which in turn help us to consider assumptions about what constitutes good teaching and about how culture shapes teacher/student patterns of interaction. For example, cultures characterised by large power distance are those that accept inequality as normal. Large power distance societies tend to have teacher-centred classrooms where the teacher is the expert; he/she is respected, and never contradicted or criticised. Students in large power-distance societies only speak when invited (Hofstede, 1986, p. 313). High uncertainty avoidance cultures feel most comfortable with clear structures, rules and parameters and less comfortable with ambiguity and unpredictability. Students from high uncertainty avoidance cultures prefer explicit instructions, need to 'know' the 'correct' answers and expect strict timelines and rules. They are frustrated by 'choose your own topic' assessments, lecturers who do not give them the answers to the exams and the concept of 'independent learning'.

We often hear from colleagues who have experienced these clashes of cultural assumptions. One, an Australian psychology lecturer, described presenting five different theoretical constructs, carefully outlining the advantages and disadvantages of each and explaining where additional information was available. The material was detailed and clearly presented. However, at the end of the lecture a number of the international students left the theatre feeling cheated. They described feeling that the lecturer had deliberately kept from them the most important piece of information: which of the methods presented was best. In addition, when the lecturer divided the class into small groups and set a series of case examples for discussion, rather than explaining the pre-set reading or outlining the conclusions he expected, many of the students felt that their lecturer was opting out of his role as teacher. Asking questions in class was not an option because they felt it would embarrass their lecturer. From their perspective, good teachers KNOW when their students are experiencing difficulty and quietly ensure that they receive the help they need.

In the previous story, each side misjudged the other. The lecturer cared deeply about teaching and had carefully prepared material to ensure his students were able to develop their understanding of a range of theoretical constructs and their contribution to the issue but from the perception of a number of his students, he was failing. The students wanted to learn but, from the lecturer's perspective, were approaching it the wrong way. Perceptions of the differences in expectations of the teacher and learner in this classroom are outlined below.

My lecturer should …   To be a good lecturer I need to …

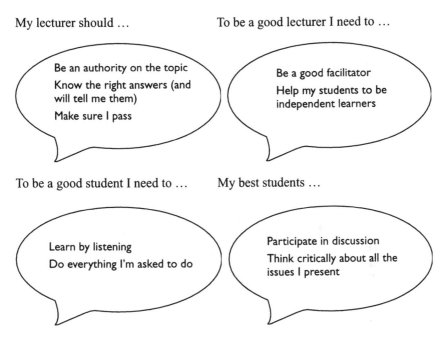

To be a good student I need to …   My best students …

Misperceptions about how we expect people to behave are important because they affect our understanding of each other. Students' expectations of what will happen in a lecture will be coloured by past experiences of their secondary school or of teaching in higher education institutions at home. A teacher may assume a student's failure to ask questions in class is because they don't know or haven't completed the reading. However, as Cortazzi and Jin (1997) observe, students face a cultural dilemma when they don't understand something explained by a lecturer. The student is concerned about losing face because they have less than perfect knowledge and there is also the implication that the teacher didn't explain properly (and the student may therefore be concerned about the teacher 'losing face'). Unwillingness to contribute in class is not just about 'losing face', it is also about feeling you have something worthwhile to contribute or expecting that you need to show a particular level of expertise. All these perceptions about appropriate behaviour in a tutorial operate within a cultural framework. Thus a lecturer can interpret the class's silence as understanding when in fact it reflects the students' respect for him or her, even though they may have understood little of the lecture. It is also worth noting that the practice of making students speak up in class is not the only way of encouraging critical thinking; silence can mean engagement in thought, not lack of ideas. The Western assumption that talking is connected to thinking is not shared in the East.

Developing intercultural competencies in classroom interaction

Cortazzi and Jin (1997) outline a number of guidelines to improve intercultural understanding in university classrooms:

1   Be aware that academic cultures (the way students and teachers interact) vary;
2   Don't transfer conclusions about a culture to an individual. Not every individual conforms to cultural trends;
3   Reflect on how communication for learning in the classroom occurs and develop an awareness of the presuppositions and cultural styles which are involved; and
4   Try to understand cultures of communication and learning and help students to understand counterpart cultures, including yours.

Particularly important is the need to 'value add', to be explicit about how and why we follow particular processes, not because one method is better than another, but to establish a framework and to provide a language for interpreting the academic culture we expect our students to work within. Supporting students in the learning process helps them develop greater awareness of the academic requirements and skills needed to achieve success.

Learning from lectures

In lectures, you will help students by clarifying aims and expectations, even if it means explaining what a literature review is and how to write one. When discussing alternative theoretical frameworks or research methods, be explicit about your expectations so that students will determine appropriateness for particular situations. When difficult or key concepts arise, paraphrase the ideas, offering several chances to understand them.

You can help students learn by considering language issues as well. You could:

* pre-teach key vocabulary and concepts, particularly technical or discipline-specific jargon (by providing lists or highlighting terms during lectures);
* avoid slang, culturally embedded references that impede understanding (Australian examples would include Toorak tractor, shout or Joe Blake)[2] and language that has pejorative connotations for the target groups, for example

Yank (for Americans), Pommy (for English) or Skip (as in Skippy the kanga-roo for Australians).

Encouraging participation in tutorials and seminars

When presenting material or leading discussion in a tutorial or seminar, you could:

* involve students (both local and international) in determining the content of a session – having some 'ownership' of what is being taught increases commit-ment (Whalley, 1997);
* organise information that is presented orally by using signposting, gestures and key visuals to show the order of importance and relationships between ideas;
* incrementalise tasks so that students can develop a foundation on which to continually build skills;
* never assume your students know what you are talking about or that you know what they are talking about ... ask.

Dealing with ideas or theoretical issues in a tutorial or seminar will be easier for all students if you:

* encourage students to think of practical uses of the theory in their own cul-tural context: how would this happen in China or Russia (or South Africa or Canada or ...)?
* ask students to give examples of recently explained theories and concepts using their own experiences.

When setting up student discussion or in-class groups:

* make the process as well as the outputs explicit, providing students with some ground rules for discussion, participation and shared responsibilities for outcomes;
* make explicit your reasons for asking questions in class and explain that you are not expecting 'perfect' answers, that errors are a part of learning;
* when asking students to 'brainstorm' a topic, explain the process, laying ground rules that all ideas are acceptable and that input from all is expected;
* allow for pair-work or small group work to facilitate conversation – all stu-dents are more likely to feel comfortable in these situations rather than having to voice opinions and discuss in a whole-class situation;
* ensure that the classroom atmosphere is respectful of input from *all* students and that you encourage responses from all.

If you are setting up tasks that students will do in groups, model both good and bad examples of assessment tasks, and follow up with analysis, discussion and short exercises (Borland and Pearce, 1999). When devolving responsibility for a task to individual students or groups, explain the pedagogical reasons for doing so.

Collaborative learning

The ability to work effectively as a team member is a highly valued skill in the global marketplace. Embedded within the curriculum in departments and taught as a professional skill at university, teamwork can also be an effective vehicle for inclusive learning. From an academic skills perspective, collaborative learning groups offer students opportunities for sharing information, reinforcing learning, peer mentoring, developing support networks and working toward a common goal. From a culture-learning perspective, collaborative groups, when set up to include multiple cultural backgrounds (as opposed to mono-cultural), can foster greater understanding and respect for different cultures, breaking down stereotyping and ethnocentric views. A study of culturally mixed groups by Volet and Ang showed that the opportunity to work together led to the realisation 'that their perceptions about peers from the other group (Australian, international) were not accurate and needed to be revised, especially the perceptions relating to language and work-related attitudes' (Volet and Ang, 1998, p. 15). A further study by Watson, Johnson and Zgourides (2002) showed that the multi-cultural teams, although at first exhibiting more individualistic behaviours, over time not only developed greater team orientation, but also outperformed mono-cultural teams – according to the authors, because they had learned to use their diversity to the advantage of the team.

Volet and Ang's (1998) study, however, also highlighted what many of us already know: students prefer to work within their own cultural groups and cross-cultural mixing does not occur spontaneously.[3] Although there are significant factors that predispose students to remain in their mono-cultural groups (for example culture distance and cultural-emotional connectedness), the benefits of developing improved cross-cultural understanding and discovering commonalities, as shown by this study as well as others (Cushner, 1994), require us to rethink our responsibility toward fostering such a learning environment.

Strategies for encouraging collaborative learning in culturally mixed groups are considered in detail in Chapters 8 and 9. Here, we mention a few aspects as a reminder that these are academic skills, too. You will help students if you:

- give them a clear rationale, based upon course objectives, course assessment and post-university outcomes, for asking them to work together: it is crucial that both local and international students perceive the task as mutually valuable;
- structure the progression of the work, beginning with small group assignments that allow students the opportunity to develop their group-based skills (negotiating, setting priorities, chunking tasks, delegating responsibility,

giving effective feedback) and leaving larger, more heavily weighted group assignments until later in the course;

* provide a set of rules as well as strategies for dealing with conflict;
* ensure that the allocation of marks is clarified prior to commencing group work; and
* provide regular opportunities for the group to demonstrate that they are on task and to receive constructive feedback.

Communicating across cultures

Oral communication skills are a fundamental aspect of academic life and key to university success. Choice of grammar and vocabulary, intonation, number and place of pauses, degree of eye contact and body language are all interpreted differently in different cultures and can therefore result in cultural misunderstandings and miscommunication. Here are some examples of how this works in practice:

'Getting to the point'

Many of the Vietnamese students at our university prefer to move straight into the main content of an issue rather than waste the time of busy academics or university administrators. This can leave a Western teacher or administrator confused by a student's lack of willingness to engage in polite conversation and they may misinterpret the behaviour as rudeness or shyness.

'Tone of voice'

Students from the Middle-East may continue to use the heavy intonation and relatively loud voices which are acceptable in Arabic with their Australian teachers. They may be interpreted by Westerners as being overbearing or aggressive or, when they begin a conversation with a context of praise for their teacher, the overture may be interpreted as inappropriate and insincere flattery (Cortazzi and Jin, 1997).

'Pauses and turn taking'

An Australian or an American observing a discussion by Greek students, where pauses between turns are minimal and overlaps between speakers considered normal, may interpret the behaviour as rude. Scandinavian students utilise slightly longer pauses as a sign of respect compared to Greek students (Cortazzi and Jin, 1997) so when they try and converse, Greeks may misinterpret the pause as a sign that they have said something wrong and Scandinavians may assume the lack of one means the Greeks are being rude.

'When to speak and when to be silent'

Asian students may interpret the willingness of students from Western backgrounds to contribute to discussion, regardless of whether they have completed the reading, as pompous. Jin and Cortazzi (1999) observe that for Chinese students, few questions are spontaneous; students do not want to waste lecturers' time and therefore questions are carefully considered before being articulated. In addition, for many students their level of language development means that they will be translating from English to their first language and then back again.

'Showing agreement'

Indian students may nod to acknowledge they are listening – not to show agreement or understanding. Japanese students can say 'yes' to indicate they hear and understand, but not necessarily to show they agree. Pausing and using 'yes' and 'no' can also be affected by the need to gain the time necessary to mentally process from a second language. Repeating a phrase can be a signal of understanding but it can also be a way of gaining more time.

Bearing in mind the opportunities for so much misunderstanding, it will encourage you and your students to be more inclusive in oral communication if you observe the way in which students talk and listen to each other and to you. Cortazzi and Jin (1997) suggest we look for and reflect on differences in:

- pausing
- turn-taking
- silences
- how opinions are shared
- how respect is shown both to peers and to authority figures.

You could also encourage working in small groups to help students gain confidence in English and discuss with students the importance of being able to operate effectively across cultures (both inside and outside the classroom).

Developing competencies in thinking and reading critically

As Borland and Pearce (1999, p. 60) note, critical thinking underpins Western academic culture and the 'reading of written text is, in a sense, the basis of tertiary study'. They also remind us that reading, unlike writing, is an invisible activity that is not generally taught in our universities, seldom if ever assessed, yet it remains effectively the key to knowledge and success at the higher education level. The ability to read critically, extract information and use sources to support an argument is highly valued in Western tertiary study, yet can mystify students, especially international students who expect their lecturers to tell them what they need to know (Australians often refer unkindly to this as 'hand-holding'). Reading, therefore, is a vital means to an end but not the end itself. When teachers comment, 'This is a great summary of the author's ideas, but what is *your* opinion?' they are signalling what they really value: the ability to use and select information.

Durkin (2004) notes that critical thinking is a universal skill but that it requires an element of intellectual humility. We must be prepared to recognise weaknesses in our own argument and it is considered inappropriate in some cultures to criticise authority figures openly or in writing. Maintaining harmony and avoiding offence is more highly valued in some cultures than the search for absolute 'truth'. Critical writing involves questioning received knowledge and reconstructing it through the writing process, and this can be at odds with some cultural learning styles. Jin and Cortazzi (1999) observe that the verb 'teach' in Chinese – *jiao shu* – literally means 'teach the book' with the teacher and textbook seen as authoritative sources of knowledge. As they note, however, with economic and social change, this culture of learning is changing and *jiao shu* is being replaced by *yu ren,* meaning 'cultivate a person', with the teacher as a model of learning.

Reading critically is a challenge for most students and most commonly they ascribe their difficulty to lack of time. Students whose second language is English can take a third to two times longer to read as first language students, often reading a text over and over to gain understanding. Because their reading is slower, second language learners tend not to read as much. Durkin (2003) recounts the experience of one of her Chinese students who said:

> I can read very quickly in Chinese. I can skim ... look at a page quickly and know what it's about. In English I have to read paragraph by paragraph.

Second language students spend a lot of time trying to understand the material with consequently less time (and confidence) available to reflect critically on it. Many students believe that they are expected to read every item on their reading list. Our experience in Australian universities suggests that students from a number of cultures (including other Western cultures) were not used to the extended reading required in even first-year subjects in Australia. In addition, little guidance is given to students about which articles to read or which chapters are important. Less emphasis is placed on extensive reading in degree courses in many Asian universities and therefore students have come to expect more guidance from a lecturer about which chapters to read. Durkin (2003) describes how one of her Hong Kong students said:

> In Hong Kong my teacher will give me a lot of knowledge without books. So I just listen.

Durkin (2003) suggests that some of the issues that can arise in reading and writing critically include:

- misunderstanding the concept of scholarly critical evaluation;
- the cultural inappropriateness of challenging scholarship for some students;
- difficulties in analysing essay questions;
- differences evident in the way different cultures structure literary texts; and
- difficulties experienced with the concept of critical reading.

In observing these difficulties, the aim is not to 'correct' a problem but to encourage awareness of the different cultural frameworks that students bring with them to class. Strategies that can be used to develop competencies in critical reading and writing include those linked to the now familiar refrain of explicitness by outlining what is required in terms of critical thought and by explaining that a reading list is not an exercise in 'reading everything'.

Lecturers can provide specific guidance and practice by:

- giving students short texts in the beginning, with guided questions that elicit the level of analysis desired;
- giving students a reading list that is both incremental in level of relevance to the area of discussion as well as complexity – the difference between basic as opposed to 'more wide-spread, professional understanding' (Borland and Pearce, 1999, p. 65);
- providing a list of key questions for students to use when reading:
  – What year was the text written? Is this relevant? Why?
  – Who wrote the text? What theoretical framework do they utilise? Do they have a particular political perspective?
  – Think about the size and nature of the sample used in research.
- modelling effective reading and critical thinking strategies in class by demonstrating them: put up several small texts on the overhead projector and evaluate them, guiding your students through your argument, opinion and supporting information;
- providing opportunities in class, both in whole- and small-group work, to critically discuss the readings.

You might encourage students to engage with the reading by asking them to:

- apply theory to practice (particularly to use practical examples from the student's own culture);
- critically engage the knowledge traditions they bring from their own cultures.

It may be helpful to avoid use of the word 'critical' at all, using instead more neutral terms such as 'compare and contrast', then as students become more able to do so, phrases such as 'explaining strengths and weaknesses of the argument'.

The culture of language: writing essays and examination assignments

Shen described the process for Chinese students learning how to write in English as learning 'not to be my Chinese self' (Shen, 1989). In writing, Chinese speakers feel the need to establish common ground and build up rapport before they lead the reader on to the main point. One Chinese student described the academic style he was used to in China 'like presenting your ideas through a delicate mist'. In China, an essay question would present the correct perspective and would not have to be analysed for assumptions and debate. It is not uncommon for students to assume the title or the key element of a question presents the argument which is accepted by the experts and therefore the one to be followed.

Such discourse styles are at odds with the expectations of British, Australian and North American academics, who approach writing in a linear style and expect an early signal of where the argument in an essay is going. Kaplan identified four structures of writing that differed from the linearity of English: circular (Chinese), digressive (Romance languages), parallel (Middle Eastern languages) and a variable of parallel (Russian and German) (as cited in Clyne, 1980). Each academic writing style is a valid form of communication within its cultural context but can be wrongly perceived in another. A French student will structure his or her writing in English according to the intellectual tradition in France; the result would be perfectly acceptable in French, but receive low marks for 'padding' and too many digressions in English. Some Western academics see the Asian preferred academic style as waffling or not getting to the point. Conversely, Jin and Cortazzi (1999) suggest that Asian students see the Western style as a 'giveaway': there is no point in reading on because the most important point is revealed in the first sentence. They also suggest it is inherently insulting to the reader, that the writer is proclaiming the obvious.

While Western academic style is more overtly linear in its logic and more explicit, in Asian academic writing the meaning is negotiated by using inference (Wilkinson and Kavan, 2003). Wilkinson and Kavan note that link words play an important role in cohesively developing the linear logic in English. Chinese does not use similar cohesive devices to link ideas between paragraphs. For this reason, some students like to use a lot of headings or subheadings in English as a form of signposting. Once students understand the value of link words they can also tend to overuse connectives (not always appropriately).

Students with lower levels of English competence often translate from English to their first language and may therefore have difficulty determining the focus of an essay or exam question. Translation is made more difficult because language is not accultural. It is ethnocentric to judge literacy skills according to any one cultural framework. As Kumaravadivelu (2003) observes, difference as deficit and difference as estrangement are unacceptably limiting perspectives. A preferable option is for multilingual students to use their own cultural background as a springboard to mastering academic discourse. Awareness of different writing values and styles can enhance rather than restrict writing competence. Kumaravadivelu suggests we should respect and value the linguistic and cultural peculiarities of our students rather than suppress them.

According to Kumaravadivelu, we can expect the following differences for students when writing in their second language:

- they do less planning at the global and local level;
- they do less goal setting and have more difficulty achieving these goals;
- organising generated material in their second language is more difficult;
- transcribing in their second language is more laborious, less fluent and less productive;
- pauses are more frequent, longer and consume more writing time;
- second language writers write more slowly and produce fewer words of text;
- writing in a second language involves less reviewing; and
- second language writers show evidence of less rereading and reflection.

Expectations about assessment are also a potential area for cross-cultural miscommunication. In Russia, for example, oral examinations are more common than written examinations, but if you were to mention the possibility of oral exams to any group of Australian students, they would visibly blanch. Expectations about assessment affect more than style; expected grades can also vary. In Australia, 50 per cent is a pass grade and marks are generally adjusted to fit a normal 'bell shaped' curve; most students can expect to fall in the 50–60 per cent range. For many students from Asia and the US, 60 per cent may be perceived as tantamount to a fail and students will be understandably distressed. One international student was devastated because she received a 'D'. For this particular course 'D' meant 'Distinction', but the student was convinced that D equalled fail. Ensuring that marking schemes are made explicit (including an indication of marks available for each section of a piece of work) and clearly explaining the overall grading system can go a long way to avoiding any misunderstandings.

Encouraging a critical approach to writing

Writing is still the major method of assessment in Western tertiary institutions, and it is not unusual for the final mark to be based almost entirely on one or two pieces of writing. This tradition is in startling contrast to other academic cultures that rely heavily on continuous assessment using a combination of short answer and multiple choice exams. Academia's dependence on writing as the sole measure of competency within the subject is a double-edged sword for many international students: on the one side, they are not used to this form of assessment; on the other, they are neither familiar with nor proficient in the skills of writing as required, for example, in Australia.

The skill of writing, like that of reading, is not necessarily explicitly taught at university. Students are expected to know how to write, or to learn by getting it wrong first and then getting help from academic skills units or tutors. Initial research about the quality of written feedback provided in distance learning shows that students value and benefit from tutor comments that were respectful of their learning situation and dynamic in their approach: explicit in nature, constructive and encouraging.

International students need to understand the importance of argument, research and supporting evidence in the construction of a standard piece of university writing. They need to realise that Western academic culture expects them to have both a 'logical' opinion that is informed by research and analysis of others' ideas and also a linear style of discourse. Therefore, follow respect with explicitness. All students can benefit from clear explanations, appropriate models and opportunities to reflect on the different writing assessment tasks expected in the course. Strategies that can be used to develop tertiary writing skills include:

- explain what 'critical thinking' is, as opposed to 'criticising';
- set clear expectations and give detailed instructions – at least in the first writing assignments;
- ask students to identify similarities and differences in academic writing conventions in their cultures as compared to yours;
- give your students examples of a lab report, literature review and reflective essay so that they can have a better understanding of what you expect;
- discuss the relevant features of the required writing, examining its different parts (introduction, body and conclusion), discourse style and purpose: argumentative, explanatory, comparative, descriptive or combinations of all;
- ask your students to identify the argument and its supporting evidence;
- give them a poorly structured essay and ask them to identify its faults and to make suggestions for improving it – use this discussion as a way to reinforce critical thinking skills and the linear style of argument preferred in English;
- give your students the opportunity to demonstrate their skills in a shorter piece of writing, and then give constructive feedback designed to elicit analysis and develop argument; and
- ask them to rewrite it so they can practise these skills.

As students develop critical writing skills and become more confident in their work, guidelines can gradually be withdrawn and independence fostered. Investing in this kind of meta-teaching throughout a course not only facilitates cross-cultural awareness while developing writing competencies, it also provides a greater assurance of achieving success from both the student's and the teacher's perspectives.

A word about cheating

Cheating is a culturally determined concept, but copying the work of other students is a strategy used by both strong and weak students world-wide and is universally motivated by a wish to get the best mark in the shortest time. Robinson and Kuin (1999) observed that Chinese students draw the boundary differently from Western university administrators and academics. They noted that Chinese learners, for example, come from a collaborative culture which values cooperation and group work. Western ideas about scholarship, including boundaries between plagiarism and cheating, are not shared by Chinese students (Scollon, 1994). Research by Evans, Craig and Mietzel (1993) suggests that German students are less likely to label certain collaborative practices as cheating than their North American counterparts. As Robinson and Kuin (1999, p. 194) note, however: 'willingness to label an activity as cheating has little to do with whether it occurs, most students say it's wrong to cheat, yet the majority say they've cheated'.

For all students, making explicit what is acceptable in terms of collaboration with peers and what is not is a valuable strategy. In Australian, British and North American classrooms, asking lecturers for help, telephoning or emailing tutors for advice, and discussing assignment topics with fellow students is acceptable classroom behaviour and generally encouraged. It is important to make this acceptable behaviour explicit to students, at the same time clearly outlining the unacceptable 'cheating' behaviours of copying all or part of another student's assignment or handing in another student's work as your own. Using terms like 'cheat sheet' sends mixed messages about cheating.

In conclusion

Academics have 'insider' knowledge; they are familiar with and understand academic conventions that few students new to university life do. In a culturally inclusive classroom, academics are aware of their own culturally influenced teaching and learning styles and 'value add' their teaching by explicitly sharing this 'insider' knowledge with their students. Culturally aware teaching is also about observing and understanding students as individuals and exploring their responses rather than judging them by ethnocentric standards. Perhaps the first strategy in developing effective intercultural competencies is to recognise that the academic skills of our international students are not necessarily 'wrong' – something often implied by comments written in red ink followed by numerous exclamation points – they are just different. Respect is crucial to negotiating effective intercultural communication and developing competencies that transcend national boundaries. By developing a framework for building intercultural competencies in our students, we prepare students for the global educational environment which is already a virtual reality through the internet and is increasingly an actual reality as numbers of international students in classrooms increase, and local students accept an international education exchange as an important aspect of university study. The framework for building intercultural competencies is relevant for all students, not a remedial short course for international students.

Notes

1 See Brislin and Yoshida (1994) for an interesting discussion about the concept of culture shock and how it should be considered a normal and even desirable part of the cross-cultural experience, rather than an 'illness' to be treated.
2 A Toorak tractor is a pejorative term for 4-wheel drive vehicle, a 'shout' is a turn for buying beers for friends (about which there are strict cultural rules) and a Joe Blake is rhyming slang for snake.
3 Volet and Ang's other significant finding from this study was that, despite the success of their mixed group experience, these students would not choose to work in culturally diverse groups in the future.

References

Baldwin, G., Jones, R. and Prince, N. (1998). *Report on Survey of International Students at the University of Melbourne*. Centre for the Study of Higher Education.

Bennett, M. J. (1988). 'Foundations of knowledge in international education exchange: Intercultural communication'. In J. M. Reid (ed.) *Building the Professional Dimension of Educational Exchange* (pp. 121–136). Yarmouth: Intercultural Press Inc.

Borland, H. and Pearce, A. (1999). *Valuing Diversity: Experiences and achievements of NESB Students at Victoria University*. Melbourne: Victoria University of Technology, Centre for Educational Development and Support.

Brislin, R. W. and Yoshida, T. (1994). 'The content of cross-cultural training: an introduction'. In W. R. Brislin and T. Yoshida (eds) *Improving Intercultural Interactions*. Thousand Oaks, CA: Sage.

Clyne, M. (1980). *Communication in a Multi-cultural Society*. Paper presented at the National Conference on Australian Society in the Multicultural 80s.

Cortazzi, M. and Jin, J. (1997). 'Communication for learning across cultures'. In D. McNamara and R. Harris (eds) *Overseas Students in Higher Education: Issues on Teaching and Learning*. London: Routledge.

Cushner, K. (1994). 'Preparing teachers for an intercultural context'. In W. R. Brislin and T. Yoshida (eds) *Improving Intercultural Interactions* (pp. 109–128). Thousand Oaks, CA: Sage.

Durkin, K. (2003). *Challenges Chinese Students Face in Adapting to Academic Expectations and Teaching/Learning Styles of UK Masters Courses: How Cross Cultural Understanding and Adequate Support Might Aid Them to Adapt*. Unpublished paper. Brisbane: University of Queensland.

Durkin, K. (2004). *The Middle Way: Exploring Differences in Academic Expectations. Perceptions of Critical Thinking of East Asian Students in the UK*. Paper presented at the International Conference on New Directions in the Humanities, Tuscany.

Evans , E. D., Craig, D. and Mietzel, G. (1993). 'Adolescents' cognitions and attributions for academic cheating'. *Journal of Psychology*, 127 (6), 796–808.

Hofstede, G. (1986). Cultural differences in teaching and learning. *International Journal of Inter-cultural Relations*, 10, 301–320.

Jin, L. and Cortazzi, M. (1999). 'The culture the learner brings: a bridge or a barrier?' In M. Byram and M. Fleming (eds) *Language Learning in Intercultural Perspective*. Cambridge: Cambridge University Press.

Kumaravadivelu, B. (2003). 'Problematizing cultural stereotypes in TESOL'. *TESOL Quarterly*, 37 (4), 609–719.

Lawrence, J. (2001). 'Academic and first year students: Collaborating to access success in an unfamiliar university culture'. *Widening Participation and Lifelong Learning: The Journal of The Institute for Access Studies and The European Access Network*, 13 (3), 1–15.

Mullins, G., Quintrell, N. and Hancock, L. (1995). 'The experiences of international and local students: three Australian universities'. *Higher Education Research and Development*, 14 (2), 202–231.

Robinson, V. M. J. and Kuin, L. M. (1999). 'The explanation of practice: Why Chinese students copy assignments'. *Qualitative Studies in Education*, 12 (2), 193–210.

Ryan, J. (2000). *A Guide to Teaching International Students*. Oxford: Oxonian Rowley Press.

Scollon, R. (1994). 'As a matter of fact: the changing ideology of authorship and responsibility in discourse'. *World Englishes*, 13 (1), 33–46.

Shen, F. (1989). 'The classroom and the wider culture: Identity as a key to learning English composition'. *College Composition and Communication*, 40 (4), 459–466.

Smart, D., Davis, D., Volet, S. and Milne, C. (1998). '*Improving social interaction between international and Australian students on university campuses*'. Report for IDP Australia (unpublished).

Volet, S. (2003). 'Challenges of internationalisation: Enhancing intercultural competence and skills for critical reflection on the situated and non-neutral nature of knowledge'. *Language and Academic Skills in Higher Education*, 6, 1–10.

Volet, S. and Ang, G. (1998). 'Culturally mixed groups on international campuses: an opportunity for inter-cultural learning'. *Higher Education Research and Development*, 17 (1), 15–23.

Watson, W., Johnson, L. and Zgourides, G. (2002). 'The influence of ethnic diversity on leadership, group process and performance: An examination of learning teams'. *International Journal of Intercultural Relations*, 26, 1–16.

Whalley, T. (1997). *Best Practice Guidelines for Internationalising the Curriculum*. British Columbia Ministry of Education, Skills and Training and the Centre for Curriculum, Transfer and Technology.

Wilkinson, L. and Kavan, H. (2003). 'Dialogues with Dragons: Helping Chinese students' academic achievement'. ATLAANZ Conference proceedings, 119–131, Vol. 8. University of Waikato: ATLAANZ.

7

Writing in the international classroom

Ms Diane Schmitt, Nottingham Trent University

International students add diversity to university classrooms because they bring with them an assortment of previous learning experiences, diverse views of the world and, in many cases, experiences of communicating and studying in more than one language. Therefore their presence in our classrooms can be a catalyst for very dynamic teaching situations. A major challenge for educators in international classrooms is finding ways to guide students from diverse backgrounds to successful attainment of the learning outcomes for any particular course or programme of study.

With regard to writing, overcoming this challenge requires instructors to think carefully about two things – the role of writing in their classrooms and the resources student writers bring to the tasks they are set. This chapter aims to specify some of the things that are known about international student writers and university level writing tasks. It will then offer guidance on how we as teachers can help our students meet our and their desired learning outcomes. Although special attention will be given to international student writers who are writing in a second language, much of what will be covered may be equally relevant to first language writers.

Second language writers (and readers)

Students who have been screened by an IELTS[1] or TOEFL[2] exam normally enter university with the minimum amount of English language needed to manage academic study. You can assume, therefore, that students' goals will be both to gain subject knowledge and to continue to acquire competence in English. However, factors other than initial competence will impact on students' ability to produce acceptable student writing. The first is their previous experience as readers and writers, with many having written very little in secondary school, even in their first language. In my conversations with international students over the years, I have learned that many students, from a variety of countries, have actually been asked to write very little in their secondary school years, even in their first language. If I ask specifically about writing in English, students regularly tell me that they have never done more than sentence-level writing. Students' previous English language reading experiences are often similarly limited. Many students will have only limited experience of reading extended texts (more than 1000 words) in English and few students will have been exposed to the range of text types they will encounter on their university courses.

A second and related factor in successful reading and writing is the size of an individual's vocabulary. Whereas a vocabulary of 40,000 words would be considered 'sufficiently large' for native English speakers, a vocabulary size of 10,000 words is generally considered large for second-language learners entering university. In a study of 643 university-aged English language students from a wide variety of countries, Schmitt, Schmitt and Clapham (2001) found an average English vocabulary size of 4,594 words. Lack of vocabulary as well as lack of control over 'known' vocabulary will slow students' reading, limit their understanding of texts and lecture input, and restrict their written output.

Language research supports the idea of a language threshold for reading and writing below which students are unable to transfer successful reading and writing skills from their first language to the second language (Grabe, 2003). Although it seems logical to set language entry requirements well above this threshold, it is not so simple. Unfortunately the threshold cannot be predetermined or simply described as a set of grammatical and lexical items. The threshold is a relative level of proficiency that will vary according to the complexity of the reading or writing task a student is set. Currie's (1993) research points out that even students who have met or exceeded the language entry requirements of their university may suffer from cognitive overload when faced with complex academic tasks. As writing task demands increase, grammatical correctness and coherence may suffer.

A third factor that may affect students' ability to produce grammatically accurate writing derives from language teaching methods in Western countries developed around a notion called *communicative competence*. Communicative competence focuses on the creation of meaning as opposed to the practice of decontextualised grammar. Anyone who has used their secondary school language skills on a holiday abroad will know that it is possible to communicate one's meaning without being grammatically accurate and that efforts to create error-free language get in the way of fluent conversation. A focus on meaning has led to a reduction in accuracy-focused instruction in many Western school and university classrooms. Finally, accuracy in second language acquisition follows a fixed sequence of development that is largely impermeable to instruction (Ellis, 1994). Teaching that follows a purely grammatical syllabus will not result in acquisition of grammatical features in the order introduced. Thus, admonitions by discipline-based teachers for students to 'do something about your grammar' need to be tempered with the knowledge that there is no quick fix when it comes to grammatical development.

University-level writing tasks

In most university courses, students face a variety of writing tasks such as quizzes, exams, essays and reports. Often, however, neither students nor lecturers are fully aware of the conceptual demands of assigned tasks or the variations in complexity across assignments. This lack of understanding can prevent students from transferring skills learned from one assignment to subsequent assignments. The fact that lecturers often lack an explicit understanding of the conceptual demands of their assignments, despite having carefully planned their course, means that students may not receive the feedback they need to acquire the skills required by the course.

Many second-language student writers (and quite possibly native speaker student writers, too) also believe in a universal idea of 'good writing'. This belief may be linked to lack of variety in previous instruction; a review of popular textbooks in English for Academic Purposes confirms that most instruction is focused on the traditional five-paragraph essay. Zhu (2004) reports a similarly narrow view amongst teachers who acknowledge differences between disciplines (e.g. assignments in Business Information Systems are different from those in Computer Science), yet expressed the belief that students who had well-developed general writing skills would be able to transfer these skills to discipline-specific writing tasks. Furthermore, most viewed teaching writing as secondary to teaching the content of their subject area and some firmly placed the responsibility for teaching writing with specialists.

Such reductionist thinking and separation of duties runs counter to findings from research, and increasingly to the practice of writing instruction. Many writing specialists view writing in the disciplines as an acculturation process which can best be fostered by situating it within, or as close to, subject-area instruction as possible. With particular regard to international students studying in preparatory English language courses, Spack (1997) questions the notion that the general language and study skills taught there can be successfully transferred to discipline-specific tasks. She argues that 'academic skills are not fixed, that academic tasks can only be understood within specific contexts, [and] that all academic work is socially situated' (Spack, 1997, p. 50). Careful consideration must then be given to how students can best be acculturated to discipline-specific discourse communities and to their writing requirements.

'Academic language ... is no one's mother tongue'

When Bourdieu and Passeron (1994, p. 8) coined the above phrase, they were highlighting the specialised nature of academic discourse. Although it is common to speak of 'the' academic community, in fact, there are many sub-communities, each with its own preferred method of communicating and language or discourse. An examination of journal abstracts for different discipline areas shows that there is considerable variation in structure as well as types of paradigms and concepts, and in the language and phrasing used. Bhatia (2002) shows that in law and business the term *case study* serves a different pedagogical purpose. Texts that share names conjure up expectations of particular textual features but *research paper, essay, examination,* or *report* may mean very different things in different disciplines (Johns, 1997). When students are studying units or courses across different discipline areas, this can cause much confusion when they switch from attendance in one unit to another, and encounter different practices, within the same day.

An important responsibility of university instructors must, therefore, be to initiate students into their subject specialisms. They need to be able to explicitly explain the daily practices of their discipline and have a means of communicating these to their students. In the case of international students, these may either complement or clash with their expectations of the tasks they are to complete or the roles they are expected to play in English-medium universities (Angelil-Carter, 2000). One example of such a clash was the case of a Brazilian PhD student for whom I was asked to provide writing support. She had been commended by her Brazilian professors for her creative use of language when she submitted her MA thesis in Portuguese. Not surprisingly then, she was aghast when her British professor sent her to me for writing support. We had many conversations in which she expressed her frustration with the requirement to strictly adhere to academic conventions that criticised her creative use of English. She felt that she was being prevented from including an important element of herself in her writing. Therefore, we can see that the instructor as mentor will need to provide a space where mismatches between student and instructor expectations can be discussed and made explicit. As our student body internationalises, we may also need to consider whether it is the academy that needs to shift its views of what constitutes good writing.

Writing from sources and the danger of plagiarism

A common mismatch of expectations occurs in the area of writing from sources. Tasks that require students to integrate reading and writing can be particularly demanding. When writing from sources, students are expected to describe and comment on the work of others using their own words. Understanding the content and significance of what has been read and knowing how to integrate this with information from other sources and one's own point of view is challenging enough for developing first-language writers. It can be doubly challenging for second-language writers who bring fewer language resources to the task.

Bound up with this inherent cognitive difficulty is the castigatory atmosphere that surrounds the notion of plagiarism. Although plagiarism is an imprecise concept with ill-defined boundaries, it is clear that it assigns ownership of words to individual writers. What is not clear is how the Western academic community expects students who do not own the words of their discipline to meet the requirements of academic assignments while they are still in the process of acquiring the language of the discipline. The quote below recalling the experiences of a Polish immigrant to Canada provides a poignant insight into what it feels like to be voiceless when the language one does know has no place in a new environment.

> The worst losses come at night ... I wait for the spontaneous flow of inner language which used to be my night time talk with myself, my way of informing the ego where the id had been. Nothing comes. Polish, in a short time, has atrophied, shrivelled from sheer uselessness. Its words don't apply to my new experiences; they are not coeval with any of the objects, or faces, or the very air I breathe in the daytime. In English, words have not penetrated to those layers of my psyche from which a private conversation could proceed. This interval before sleep used to be the time when my mind became both receptive and alert, when images and words rose up to consciousness, reiterating what had happened during the day, adding the day's experiences to those already stored there, spinning out the thread of my personal story.
>
> Now, this picture-and-word show is gone; the thread has been snapped. I have no interior language, and without it, interior images – those images through which we assimilate the external world, through which we take it in, love it, make it our own – become blurred too.
>
> (Hoffman, 1989, pp. 107–108)

Students need to assimilate new knowledge gleaned from their academic studies with previous knowledge and experience. A lack of their own words to express their ideas is the most common reason students give for their reliance on the language of their texts in their writing. Therefore, while purchasing papers over the internet or copying with the intent to deceive is clearly plagiarism, it is less clear that borrowing the words of others in an attempt to find one's own voice in a new language should implicate one in a criminal act. The following paragraphs aim to examine the notion of plagiarism with regard to developing second-language writers from three points of reference – language, ideas and culture.

Language acquisition and plagiarism

Angelil-Carter (2000, p. 2) explains that

> underlying the concept of plagiarism is the basic premise that meaning is made by the individual, using the system of language at his or her disposal. The words and ideas thus originated then belong to the individual who first thought of them, or who first used these words in a particular way.

This notion is problematic from a linguistics point of view as Pawley and Syder (1983) argue that native speaker fluency is derived not from creative language use, but from the use of a shared set of memorised stock phrases that native speakers understand and tacitly agree are the most efficient and thus expected ways of expressing ideas. These formulaic phrases number in the hundreds of thousands and are readily understood in ways that creative language use would not be, as shown in the following example.

Stock phrases:

Opponents of this position argue that plagiarism *should not automatically be viewed as* the intention to deceive.

vs.

An attempt at creative language use:

Those who challenge this stance declare that it ought not to be considered that deception is always the aim of a student who has been accused of plagiarising.

Language acquisition is not about creatively developing one's own idiosyncratic method of speaking or writing; rather, it is about learning to use the conventionalised language of the community one finds oneself in and learning to appropriate others' language to establish group membership. Hull and Rose (1989) point out that 'a fundamental social and psychological reality about discourse – oral *or* written – is that human beings continually appropriate each other's language to establish group membership, to grow, and to define themselves in new ways' (1989, p.151). It is precisely the use of non-conventionalised language that marks international students out as non-native speakers and, potentially, as marginalised members of their disciplinary community.

Ideas and plagiarism

Copying words is a relatively straightforward view of plagiarism, but claims that ideas have been copied are more problematic because different writers may come to the same or similar conclusions through different routes. As I delve deeper into the literature on plagiarism for the purposes of writing this chapter, I, myself, am finding that many of my own 'novel' ideas about second-language writers writing from sources have been extensively discussed by others in the literature. Students as newcomers to their disciplines will often have difficulty distinguishing between their own understandings, common knowledge in a particular field, and specific viewpoints or findings. This can make it difficult to identify individual student writers' voices or viewpoints in their writing and it also makes it difficult for students to maintain coherence in their writing.

I got so easily a clear idea of how to improve my draft. Then I began to put my own voice in my writing. I didn't know, however, how to organize the writing with my own opinion. It caused disorder in my draft. When I presented only information and other people's ideas, at least people can understand what was written, even though they could not understand what I was going to say about it. It is like swimming with no breaths. I can swim effectively as long as I do not breathe. But once I take a breath, my swimming will break down completely. In the same way, my writing broke down as soon as I put in my voice.

(Cadman, 1997, pp. 9–10).

Learning to write from the sources of a specific discipline is an acculturation process into that discipline. It can be extremely difficult for students to reference effectively until they have spent a considerable amount of time reading around the discipline to understand its key concepts, theoretical underpinnings, values and controversies. Requiring first-year undergraduates to write about a new discipline *in their own words* is distinctly problematic when knowledge of the discipline is anything but their own.

Therefore, our expectations of students' writing need to take account of the stages of development students will go through as new initiates into their respective discourse communities. Wilson (1997, cited in Dudley-Evans, 2002, p. 234)

suggests that that there are four stages in the development of academic writing. These are *repetition*, which involves extensive copying without citation; *patching*, which also involves extensive copying but with appropriate citations; *plagiphrasing*, in which students blend copied sections, quotations, paraphrases, and their own words; and, finally, *conventional academic writing* … [T]he third stage, plagiphrasing, shows that students are beginning to speak with their own voices, and is an important stage on the way to developing the appropriate academic writing style.

Learning stage continuum

no citation ⟶ over-citation ⟶ appropriate citation

These four stages may be viewed as a continuum such as the one above. In order for students to be able to move along this continuum, they will need a considerable amount of practice with writing from textual sources. They will also need clear feedback on their progress.

Culture and plagiarism

Although cultural reasons are given to explain why some students from some countries appear to borrow text more than others, most students I have met understand the concept of plagiarism regardless of where they come from. They may not, however, understand the specifics of what is considered to constitute plagiarism or may consider it a valid writing strategy.

Students often try to 'guess' what their teachers want and try to avoid making 'mistakes' by copying extensively from the course text by weaving sentences and phrases from various parts of the texts together into their own work. While marking MA dissertations this summer, I noticed that my international students' writing was more stylistically appropriate and linguistically accurate in the literature review section than in the results or discussion sections. Looking at the work more carefully, I realised that the students had used the language from the literature review texts as a scaffold and this resulted in more academic sounding prose. When they wrote up, analysed and discussed their results they had no scaffold so there were more instances of awkward phrasing and grammatical inaccuracy.

Hull and Rose (1989, p.149) point out that 'negative injunctions' such as the dire warnings often given about the penalties for plagiarising leave a strong impression on developing writers. When students are advised to avoid particular behaviours without an understanding of why or what else they should do, they will try to find their own ways of making sense of what is expected of them. When these ways do not match the expectations of their teachers, students may be negatively evaluated.

A final point about plagiarism, language use and ideas is related to the decision processes assessors go through when making a judgement about whether or not a student has plagiarised. Teachers have a number of indicators that generate suspicions of plagiarism. These can include a student's in-class participation, knowledge of a student's background, previous work handed in by the student, as well as shifts in style in the writing being marked. Angelil-Carter (2000) expresses concern that false assumptions may be made about a student's ability to hold and express sophisticated ideas or to stretch to a higher level of language use on a given occasion if they are writing in a second language. As teachers, we must remember that even weak language users and second-language writers are capable of possessing and developing sophisticated ideas and language. We must take care not to fall into the trap of searching for weaknesses in our students' writing as proof that they haven't plagiarised instead of looking out for their strengths.

Guiding students toward successful learning

Armed with a greater understanding of the task facing international student writers, teachers need to consider their role in facilitating a student's subject learning and writing development. Even if one takes the view that the discipline specialist's role is to teach the subject, we must also acknowledge that assessment of that subject knowledge is dependent on the production of specific types of texts that themselves require development of a particular set of skills. We might lament that students are not up to the academic tasks we set, or that students have not got the academic skills they need. However, within this lament we find a contradiction – why are we setting tasks that students do not have the skills to achieve? Although we can say that it is the students' responsibility to develop these skills, we must own up to the fact that it is our responsibility to set achievable goals and ensure that students know exactly what is expected to achieve them. The following are some ideas about how teachers can fulfil their responsibility.

1 Get ready to collaborate

Find out who runs your English language unit, your writing centre and/or your learning and teaching enhancement unit. Enlist their help in identifying the literacy skills that underpin your discipline. Building partnerships between discipline specialists and literacy specialists makes everyone's skills and knowledge go further. These partnerships can be informal partnerships in which there is a sharing of information about a course or programme. This sharing can generate ideas as to how the needs of second-language writers could be better catered for. Alternatively, more formal partnerships could be developed which include collaborative curriculum development and even delivery.

2 Find out early what your students can do and what they cannot do (or are not aware of) with regard to academic writing in your discipline

Set an early diagnostic task that includes some of the basic skills that students will need to use in credit-bearing assignments. If students have gaps in their skills set, then look at ways of building some teaching into your course or identify language or study skills sessions that students can attend, stressing the importance of attendance.

3 Clarify your expectations for the academic genres in your discipline

Identify clearly for yourself and for your students the characteristics of a good assignment in your discipline. Try to provide examples of previous students' work to represent different types of approaches and point out why they are successful. Show students different examples for different types of assignment tasks. Indicate the types of materials and sources that should be researched and included, and the approximate number of sources that should be included (indicating a notional minimum and maximum figure).

4 Head off cognitive overload

Evaluate the complexity of the tasks you set, perhaps using the list below to judge their difficulty:

- the level of abstraction required
- the number of activities or operations involved
- the guidance provided by the prompt

- the amount of text to be assimilated
- the expected genre, and the student's prior knowledge (Currie, 1993, p. 112).

Is the level of difficulty appropriate for the students' level and the stage of the course? Is the amount of guidance appropriate to the complexity of the task? Compare your tasks with those of colleagues teaching at the same or at higher or lower levels. Make any necessary adjustments to your tasks. Complex tasks should not be avoided, but achievement levels can be increased if such tasks are broken down into a series of steps with feedback provided at each stage. Feedback is most effective when it is provided at intermediary stages of the writing process so that students can respond to it in subsequent revisions.

5 Remember that international students are still language learners and set realistic standards for their language use

All students have issues relating to the newness of the language of their academic discipline, but Shaw and Liu (1998) report that students are likely to exhibit three kinds of linguistic problems – inappropriacy, inaccuracy and lack of linguistic resources. Evidence suggests that second-language writers will make most progress with inappropriacy. An emphasis on accuracy may result in students copying for fear of making mistakes. Good writers prioritise meaning over form. It is a characteristic of weak writers to give priority to form and this can have a paralysing effect on writing fluency.

6 Provide incentives for your students to read

The problem of university students not keeping up with their assigned readings is a classic one. However, for international students, whether or not they read widely in their subject area can be a crucial factor in their success. Extensive reading contributes not only to improved fluency in reading, but it can also contribute to improvements in vocabulary, grammar and writing. Reading also provides insights into the written academic style that students do not get from lectures or classroom discussions.

Develop ways to bring the reading into the classroom. New words and concepts can be discussed and students can be encouraged to keep a glossary of new terms. Students' prior knowledge can be made explicit through questioning techniques as part of the discussion of readings and this can be used to connect to the new meanings and knowledge required. Make a point of discussing reading assignments and allow time for questions about the readings. If students think you care whether they read or not, it can make a big difference in whether or not they put in the time and effort. If you are able to develop a linked teaching arrangement such as that discussed in point 1 above, course readings can be examined closely to raise awareness of specific language use.

7 Build in practice in writing

All student writers benefit from opportunities to practise particular types of text. This will be especially true for second-language writers who need to balance both language and task-specific demands. Providing more than one assessment point per class gives students more than one chance to try out their skills and timely feedback means students can incorporate your suggestions into future assignments. Also, find out what other types of assignments your students are doing for their other classes. Look for ways for skill-building to be a cross-programme endeavour.

8 Use examples of student copying as a prompt for instruction

Make sure that students understand the purpose of citation and referencing. Draw students' attention to how and why referencing is used in your discipline. Have students compare their own use of references with that of other writers in the discipline. Make clear that writing for pedagogical purposes may require referencing of information that might be considered common knowledge for someone more expert in the field.

9 Recognise that poor writing may simply be evidence of weaknesses in other literacy skills – understanding lectures, critical reading, or learning from oral discussions

In conclusion, we need to think of university students as learners of both disciplinary knowledge and ways of doing. The 'ways of doing' requires learning the skill set expected of any member of a particular academic community, whether it is biology or cultural studies. It also requires developing the conventionalised language of the members of that academic community. For international students who use English as a second language, there may be additional skills and language to be mastered. By thinking carefully about how we design the learning activities in our courses, we can better serve the needs of all of our students.

Notes

1 International English Language Testing System (IELTS)
2 Test of English as a Foreign Language (TOEFL) – a new version of TOEFL will go live in September 2005.

References

Angelil-Carter, S. (2000). *Stolen Language*. Harlow, UK: Longman.
Bhatia, V. (2002). 'A generic view of academic discourse'. In J. Flowerdew, *Academic Discourse*. Harlow, UK: Longman.

Bourdieu, P. and Passeron, J.-C. (1994). 'Introduction: Language and the relationship to language in the teaching situation'. In P. Bourdieu, J.-C. Passeron and M. de Saint Martin, *Academic Discourse*. Cambridge: Polity Press.

Cadman, K. (1997). 'Thesis writing for international students: A question of identity?'. *English for Specific Purposes*, 16, 3–14.

Currie, P. (1993). 'Entering a disciplinary community: Conceptual activities required to write for one introductory university course'. *Journal of Second Language Writing*, 2, 101–117.

Dudley-Evans, T. (2002). 'The teaching of the academic essay: Is a genre approach possible?' In A. Johns, *Genre in the Classroom*. Mahwah, N.J.: Lawrence Erlbaum Associates.

Ellis, R. (1994). *The Study of Second Language Acquisition*. Oxford: Oxford University Press.

Grabe, W. (2003). 'Reading and writing relations: Second language perspectives on research and practice'. In. B. Kroll (ed.), *Exploring the Dynamics of Second Language Writing*. New York: Cambridge University Press.

Hoffman, E. (1989). *Lost in Translation*. New York: Penguin Books.

Hull, G. and Rose, M. (1989). 'Rethinking remediation: Toward a social-cognitive understanding of reading and writing'. *Written Communication*, 6, 139–155.

Johns, A. (1997). *Text, Role and Context*. New York: Cambridge University Press.

Pawley, A. and Syder, F. (1983). 'Two puzzles for linguistic theory: Nativelike selection and nativelike fluency'. In J.C. Richards and R. Schmidt, *Language and Communication*. London: Longman.

Schmitt, N., Schmitt, D. and Clapham, C. (2001). 'Developing and exploring the behaviour of two new versions of the Vocabulary Levels Test'. *Language Testing*, 18, 55–88.

Shaw, P. and Liu, E. (1998). 'What develops in the development of second-language writing'. *Applied Linguistics*, 19, 225–254.

Spack, R. (1997). 'The acquisition of academic literacy in a second language: A longitudinal case study'. *Written Communication*, 14, 3–62.

Zhu, W. (2004). 'Faculty views on the importance of writing, the nature of academic writing, and teaching and responding to writing in the disciplines'. *Journal of Second Language Writing*, 13, 29–48.

8

Fostering intercultural learning through multicultural group work

Mr Glauco De Vita, Oxford Brookes University

It is becoming increasingly clear that despite paying lip service to various aspects of internationalisation, many higher education institutions keen to increase recruitment of international students and expand their financial base are failing to make the most of the opportunities that student diversity provides: promoting genuine internationalism and fostering intercultural learning. Wright and Lander (2003) recently commented on the difference between having a culturally diverse student population and having those students engaged in positive interaction by stating that 'universities are deluding themselves if they believe that the presence of international students on campus contributes to the internationalisation of higher education' (p. 250). In short, the rhetoric of education internationalisation hides the fact that intercultural interaction, in and outside the classroom, is not developing naturally, and is at best limited, among students from culturally diverse backgrounds.

Evidence attesting to this problem is now ubiquitous. Despite Elsey's (1990) claim that the 'human contact' elements of education are seen as important by both home and international students, home and international students do not spontaneously mix. Research in Australia (Volet and Ang, 1998) revealed that home students tend to prefer low levels of interaction with international students, particularly those from Asian backgrounds. This was also observed in the UK (Thom, 2000), and in German universities, where over half of the home students do not appear to experience any real contact with European (Erasmus) exchange students (Bargel, 1998, cited in Otten, 2003).

This suggests that the ideal of transforming a culturally diverse student population into a valued resource for activating processes of international connectivity, social cohesion and intercultural learning is still very much that, an ideal. Following the US model, most attempts at curriculum internationalisation have been based on the idea that it can be achieved by means of the mere infusion of some international materials in existing course syllabi. By stressing the role of knowledge dissemination in the learning process, the infusion approach overlooks the genetic make-up of intercultural learning (see De Vita and Case, 2003). Intercultural learning is not just about acquiring new knowledge at the cognitive level, it requires participation in social experiences that stimulate learning also in the self and action domains. It involves the discovery and transcendence of difference through authentic experiences of cross-cultural interaction that involve real tasks, and emotional as well as intellectual participation.

Institutions and educators interested in genuine internationalisation of higher education can create curricular spaces which foster intercultural learning through multicultural group work. The opportunities to create authentic intercultural learning encounters through multicultural group work can:

- counter the predominantly ethnocentric approach to higher education found in most university systems (Furnham and Bochner, 1982);
- prepare students to function in an international and intercultural context (Knight and de Wit, 1995);
- enhance all students' understanding and appreciation of other cultures (Volet and Ang, 1998);
- challenge cultural stereotypes and send an unambiguous message of equality to students (De Vita, 2000); and
- promote intercultural communication as a critical process of making meanings, of sharing meanings, and of building bridges across multiple realities and multiple truths (Fox, 1996; Hellmundt, 2003).

These educational goals are not merely instrumental to the development of intercultural competencies dictated by changes in the demographic and cultural composition of our societies and the new requirements of the world of work. Collectively, they form an agenda of social responsibility in fostering greater understanding, tolerance and respect among all people. They convey a message aimed at instigating a genuine process of cultural exchange intended to empower students to participate effectively in a free society; a society in which cultural, linguistic, ethnic and racial diversity are seen as a source of enrichment rather than as a problem, and inequality and discrimination are not only resisted but actively challenged.

Facilitating the multicultural group work experience

Forming the groups

Many students hold negative preconceptions about group work (Shanka and Napoli, 2001) and generally do not look forward to cooperative learning activities that are formally assessed. Ledwith *et al.* (1996) show how this problem is even more pronounced in the context of teamwork involving culturally mixed groups, with home students displaying strong preferences for working with students like themselves.

Sadly, in practice, tutors' response to these attitudes has predominantly been that of allowing students to self-select the composition of the groups; a convenient option for those lecturers who don't wish to risk becoming unpopular with their students. Of course, the problem with this approach is that by encouraging students to build on their existing networks, it does not promote social cohesion. It follows that culturally mixed groups must be engineered by the tutor if intercultural contact as part of formal study is to take place.

Interestingly, the report by Ledwith *et al.* (1996) also drew attention to the potential cause of the tension between home and international students in completing assessed projects in culturally mixed groups:

> the emphasis of the UK students was on their individual current average mark, that group work tended to pull this down, and the fear that this would impact adversely on their final degree classification
>
> (p.6)

Assessed multicultural group work can be a poor reflector of individual abilities and, because of this, can lead to resentment among students. The fair assessment of individuals participating in group work is not unique to cross-cultural groups, but merits special consideration in multicultural settings if both home and international students are to enthusiastically participate in the learning experience.

In my investigations within my own teaching, I found that multicultural group work has, on average, a positive rather than negative effect on the individual average mark of all students. Such findings need to be shared with students to remove false and stereotypical preconceptions that may hinder the development of educationally rich and rewarding intercultural interactions amongst students.

Preparing students for the difficulties ahead

Working collaboratively is particularly difficult in multicultural educational settings. It is, therefore, important to help students recognise that although the group work experience can be very exciting and rewarding, it will present cultural challenges that are both socially and emotionally demanding.

To appreciate the potential impact that even the most subtle cultural differences can have on intra-group dynamics, consider the issue of communication of emotion. Although classic research assumed that the expression and recognition of emotion are largely universal, more recent work (e.g. Matsumoto, 1989) has revealed that while we all share a basic common affect programme governing emotional communication, some display and decoding rules follow culturally specific norms that can create a real barrier to effective communication.

Unlike monocultural groups, where the many cultural assumptions shared by members help to shape the norms of the group and enable it to function, members of multicultural groups also have to confront differences in beliefs and expectations about the interplay of the 'self' and the 'we' of group life, about norms of communication between members, and about the way in which decisions are reached. For example, in some cultures, individuals operating in a group are expected to subordinate the self-interest to the well-being of the collective, while in other cultures, the emphasis on the individual is preserved, and teamwork is merely seen as the vehicle through which individual skills and competencies are combined to achieve a common goal (Smith and Berg, 1997).

Perhaps even more important is that each member's communicative participation in any given interaction with others is bound to be influenced by his or her cultural orientation. In some cultures, someone who is intense, talkative, employs direct communication and doesn't miss an opportunity to subject ideas to critical scrutiny would be regarded as the ideal group member. In other cultures, diplomacy, tactfulness and a certain degree of inhibition associated with the concept of 'face' (defined by Watson, 1999, as the consequences of episodes leading to the loss of self-esteem or respect for others) are seen as essential group-based skills. Often the problems stemming from these different cultural orientations manifest themselves not so much in mis-communication but in lack of communication. Wright and Lander (2003) investigated the verbal communication behaviours of Australian and South East Asian students in mono-ethnic and bi-ethnic group settings and found that, in the presence of Australian students, South East Asian students were inhibited in terms of their frequency of verbal interactions. They also established that this finding could not be fully accounted for by lack of language proficiency per se, and suggested that Australian students' verbal dominance may have placed them in a position of authority that allowed them to assume a dominant role. It is important to recognise that here it is not the fear of making face-threatening linguistic errors that is seen as leading to the hierarchical role differentiation. This asymmetry of communicative power may have originated from a range of other factors (sociolinguistic competence, knowledge of the interactive norms of the 'host' culture, etc.) that, coupled with a well-defined 'power distance' orientation, may have made it much more difficult for the South East Asian students to assert themselves. In this context, therefore, they might have been culturally inclined to assume a submissive, more silent role. Interestingly, the interpretation of silence too has cultural connotations that make it difficult to distinguish silences meant to convey understanding and approval from silences of uncertainty or disagreement (Cortazzi and Jin, 1997). Jones (1999) provides an insightful analysis of cross-cultural relativity in the evaluation of silence which highlights how while in some cultures 'not speaking' may be interpreted as a way of concealing the truth and being uncooperative, in other cultures silence is regarded as a highly valued moral virtue that helps to promote group harmony.

It is not difficult to see at this point how different cultural dispositions towards collectivity, diplomacy, response to authority and the interpretation of silence may also determine, and possibly shift, the centre of gravity of group processes taking place along the autocratic-participative locus of decision-making.

Although by no means intended to provide a comprehensive review of the challenges associated with the added dimension of cultural diversity, the above examples help us to recognise how unresolved cultural differences can give rise to misunderstandings, anxiety and emotional distress. Such tensions may add to those stemming from the multiplicity of identities (class, race, gender, etc.) that each individual brings to the group. Within these tensions and differences, however, lies the potential for authentic multicultural learning encounters. Ignoring them would make the whole experience meaningless and could ultimately lead to conflict. Since modes of conflict resolution too vary from culture to culture, this may seriously disrupt the cohesiveness of the group.

Designing the task

Whilst recognising that learning to accept the varied ways of being and doing is, ultimately, an outcome associated with an individual's choice of personal transformation and development, properly conceived tasks can play an important function in facilitating students' discovery and transcendence of difference. But what makes for a properly conceived task in order to promote intercultural learning? First, the task should be designed so as to explicitly call for students' exploration of their cultural identities, and of their current perceptions of these.

O'Dowd's (2003) intercultural learning project involving a technology-mediated exchange between Spanish and English learners provides a powerful example of the potential that lies in effective design. Following the components of Byram's (1997) model of intercultural competence, he set a series of tasks aimed at increasing students' cultural awareness. The tasks (ten in total) included word association exercises, the evaluation of cultural portraits embedded in traditional narratives, and reciprocal (emic and etic) interpretative analyses of cultural products and practices. In reporting on the extent to which the tasks succeeded in making students more aware of their own culture and how it was viewed by the members of the foreign culture, O'Dowd wrote:

> Students told anecdotes, expressed theories, and made assumptions about the foreign culture, and then looked for their partners to respond to these ideas by either confirming or denying them. In this way students constructed a new perspective towards the other culture or, at times, simply confirmed their old one.
>
> (O'Dowd, 2003: 133)

In my own task design, I encourage cooperative intercultural inquiry where students combine the roles of both researcher and object to generate a 'creative tension' that can be channelled towards the collective purpose of the group. I ask student groups to give examples of stereotypical images of their culture, and subject these portraits to critical scrutiny and factual verification. The result is that we all become more conscious of our own stereotypical beliefs and consequently become more eager to learn the actual differences in what Hofstede (1984: 21) refers to as 'the collective programming of the mind which distinguishes the members of one human group from another'.

Notwithstanding the initial discomfort experienced by students as they come to see distorted and at times offensive images of their cultures through the eyes of the 'Other', tasks of this nature help students realise that to combat national stereotyping we should start from ourselves since we are all, perhaps subconsciously or unintentionally, burdened with stereotypical beliefs.

In conceiving the task, the tutor should also consider how the contributions of individuals are likely to contribute to the group's outcome. By setting tasks that fail to require input from every group member, tutors inadvertently foster social loafing (Michaelsen et al., 1997). It follows that, especially in the context of culturally mixed groups, the project should be one which, by making division of labour difficult, promotes interdependence, broad-based participation, and the use of the varied cultural perspectives that different students bring to the group.

The benefits of diversity can be further induced through tasks which help reveal that the needs, values and perspectives of members of different cultural groups are potentially complementary rather than mutually exclusive. 'Productive cultural diversity' (Cope and Kalantzis, 1997) can flourish, and more effective outcomes achieved through cultural synergy.

Providing guidance on group processes

Facilitating the development of cohesive multicultural groups is not just about effective task design; it also entails providing guidance to students on how to find a common approach to working together. Such approaches need to be driven by a group culture characterised by mutual respect, trust and a genuine commitment to integration. Group members need to feel safe in expressing their views and make sure that the ideas of all members are heard before any are evaluated. Members should be able to feel safe in questioning the views of others and establish mechanisms for critique and evaluation within a supportive rather than personally threatening climate that is conducive to multicultural feedback. These conditions could be formally operationalised by means of agreed group processes aimed at 'de-centering', the exploration of what each cultural perspective has to offer, and 're-centering', the integration of the strengths of each (Maznevski and Peterson, 1997).

Specific strategies to be adopted in circumstances where group decisions cannot be reached through consensus (compromise, majority voting, etc.) should also be negotiated by group members. Additionally, groups should be advised to elect a 'chair' or 'facilitator', who acts as guardian of these processes and is responsible for performing group maintenance functions (encouraging, eliciting participation, energising, harmonising, etc.). This could be a rotating role, so that no group member is denied the opportunity to develop and practise such skills. Most importantly, students should be reassured that the exploration and appreciation of difference can be achieved without undermining their own cultural status, role and identity, since what is looked for is not the homogenisation of difference, or even worse, the adaptation of the 'guest' to the culture of the 'host', but a true, open dialogue aimed at reaching greater understanding (Fox, 1997).

Adopting an appropriate style

The tutor is likely to adopt a range of styles during the life of the group from taking full responsibility to being fully facilitative, allowing the group to operate autonomously. The art lies in balancing and sequencing tutor behaviours in accordance with the stages of development of the group. During the initial formation stage, the optimal mode is often hierarchical, providing a clear framework within which early collaboration can develop. Later, some degree of control is released to the groups and a more cooperative approach in devising learning processes is set in place. Finally, with a fully matured, cohesive group, the only task expected of the facilitator is that of allowing the groups' self-determination and self-direction to flourish.

Helping students to make sense of the multicultural encounter

Providing opportunities for intercultural interaction and offering guidance on how to deal with the complexities inherent in multicultural group work and facilitate the development of a cohesive group are necessary but not sufficient conditions for intercultural learning. Indeed, Otten (2003) warns that without reflection, cross-cultural experiences risk emphasising foreignness and the differences between cultures; they may even augment existing stereotypes and prejudices. By prompting learners to re-evaluate and reflect, tutors assist students in making sense of the experience, in developing new attitudes and competencies, and in expanding the way in which they view themselves, others and the world. Reflection can be difficult to teach and practise as it requires higher-order cognitive skills such as the ability to envisage alternative behavioural scenarios. Often students are not prepared for the feelings that might be involved and this is one of the reasons that reflection is not perceived as enjoyable.

Some of these difficulties can be eased by anticipating the challenges ahead, and by being clear about the kind of learning we wish to promote. Is reflection meant to help students 'look back' at the experience and reach conclusions that can inform and improve future action? Is it an introspective exercise aimed at encouraging learners to hold up the 'mirror' of self-reflection? Or is it intended to be a 'window' that looks out, and encourages careful observing of, and attendance to, foreign meanings and interpretations? In the context of intercultural learning, reflection should be all of the above. You can ask students questions about where the beliefs and behaviours that characterised the multicultural encounter came from. Did students notice communication patterns, interplays of power, fulfilled and unfulfilled expectations? This type of reflection demands curiosity, openness and honesty in attending to the feelings (positive and negative) evoked by the multicultural encounter. Students will be more willing to be candid and honest if these are explicitly included in the criteria adopted for the assessment of the reflective component.

Conclusions

Financially driven expansion of international recruitment does not, in itself, lead to opportunities for intercultural interaction among students. Rather than reducing intercultural learning to an unproblematic increase in the learners' knowledge, institutions and educators committed to genuine internationalisation of the curriculum should be concerned with providing spaces for experiences that involve all senses and levels of learning, and multicultural group work presents itself as the ideal vehicle for activating the social, behavioural and emotional learning processes that are required to develop an internationalised culture.

Multicultural group work provides opportunities for fostering intercultural learning but it must involve careful attention to processes of group formation and awareness of the complexities and difficulties involved in intercultural work. Effective group tasks, helping students to develop cohesive multicultural groups, and the facilitation of group work are also vital ingredients for successful multicultural group work. We need to be clear about the intercultural outcomes we wish to promote, and ensure that all the elements of the cooperative learning framework we employ – from task design to assessment – are consistent with one another in promoting that learning.

References

Byram, M. (1997). *Teaching and Assessing Intercultural Communicative Competence*. Clevedon, England: Multilingual Matters.

Cortazzi, M. and Jin, L. (1997). 'Communication for learning'. In D. McNamara and R. Harris (eds) *Overseas Students in Higher Education*. London: Routledge.

Cope, B. and Kalantzis, M. (1997). *Productive Diversity*. Annandale: Pluto Press.

De Vita, G. (2000) 'Inclusive approaches to effective communication and active participation in the multicultural classroom: an international business management context'. *Active Learning in Higher Education*, 1, 168–180.

De Vita, G. and Case, P. (2003). 'Rethinking the internationalisation agenda in UK higher education'. *Journal of Further and Higher Education, 27*, 383–398.

Elsey, B. (1990). 'Teaching and learning'. In M. Kinnell (ed.) *Learning Experiences of Overseas Students* (pp. 46–62). Milton Keynes: The Society for Research into Higher Education and Open University Press.

Fox, C. (1996). 'Listening to the other: Mapping intercultural communication in postcolonial educational consultancies'. In R. Paulston (ed.) *Social Cartography. Mapping Ways of Seeing Social and Educational Change*. London: Garland Publishing.

Fox, C. (1997) 'The authenticity of intercultural communication'. *International Journal of Intercultural Relations, 21*, 85–103.

Furnham, A. and Bochner, S. (1982). *Culture Shock: Psychological Reactions to Unfamiliar Environments*. London: Methuen.

Hellmundt, S. (2003). '*Theory and practice: Strategies to promote intercultural communication among international and local students*'. Unpublished discussion paper.

Hofstede, G. (1984). *Culture's Consequences*. London: Sage Publications.

Jones, J. (1999). 'From silence to talk: Cross-cultural ideas on students' participation in academic group discussion'. *English for Specific Purposes,* 18, 243–259.

Knight, J. and de Wit, H. (1995). 'Strategies for internationalisation of higher education: Historical and conceptual perspectives'. In H. de Wit (ed.) *Strategies for Internationalisation of Higher Education: A Comparative Study of Australia, Canada, Europe and the United States of America.* Amsterdam: European Association for International Education.

Ledwith, S., Lee, A., Manfredi, S. and Wildish, C. (1996). *Multiculturalism, Student Group Work and Assessment.* Oxford: Oxford Brookes University.

Matsumoto, D. (1989) 'Cultural influences on the perception of emotion'. *Journal of Cross-Cultural Psychology,* 20, 92–105.

Maznevski, M. and Peterson, M. (1997). 'Societal values, social interpretation, and multi-national teams'. In C. Granrose and S. Oskamp (eds) *Cross-cultural Work Groups.* London: Sage.

Michaelsen, L.K., Fink, L.D. and Knight, A. (1997). 'Designing effective group activities: Lessons for classroom teaching and faculty development'. In D. De Zure (ed.) *To Improve the Academy.* Stillwater, OK: New Forum Press and the Professional and Organisational Development Network in Higher Education.

O'Dowd, R. (2003). 'Understanding the "other side": Intercultural learning in a Spanish – English e-mail exchange'. *Language Learning and Technology,* 7, 118–144.

Otten, M. (2003) 'Intercultural learning and diversity in higher education'. *Journal of Studies in International Education,* 7, 12–26.

Shanka, T. and Napoli, J. (2001). *Learning through group projects: The student perspective.* Paper presented at the *World Marketing Congress,* Cardiff University, Cardiff, June.

Smith, K. and Berg, D. (1997). 'Cross-cultural groups at work'. *European Management Journal,* 15, 8–15.

Thom, V. (2000). 'Promoting intercultural learning and social inclusion for international students'. In B. Hudson and M. Todd (eds) *Internationalising the Curriculum in Higher Education: Reflecting on Practice.* Sheffield: Sheffield Hallam University Press.

Volet, S. and Ang, G. (1998). 'Culturally mixed groups on international campuses: an opportunity for inter-cultural learning'. *Higher Education Research and Development,* 17, 5–23.

Watson, D. (1999). '"Loss of face" in Australian classrooms'. *Teaching in Higher Education,* 4, 355–362.

Wright, S. and Lander, D. (2003). 'Collaborative group interactions of students from two ethnic backgrounds'. *Higher Education Research and Development,* 22, 237–252.

9

Multicultural groups for discipline-specific tasks

Can a new approach be more effective?

Ms Jude Carroll, Oxford Brookes University

As Western universities admit more international students, the one place where students from a range of cultural backgrounds are likely to encounter each other is when asked to work together in groups. By setting group tasks, teachers create the nexus where student diversity can challenge the learning opportunities for all members of the group and provide a chance for them genuinely to learn from and with each other as described in Chapter 8. In the previous chapter, the author described how the group's task itself focused on students' cultural difference. Whilst not as straightforward as the many issues raised made clear, this kind of group work at least makes explicit the international and intercultural dimensions of the task and foregrounds the students' cultural backgrounds.

In contrast, this chapter addresses group tasks which require several weeks or more of student effort without teacher supervision, which result in a grade or mark and which address learning outcomes linked to the discipline or the syllabus. This chapter builds on all the suggestions made in the previous chapter and considers how to manage and assess students doing discipline-specific tasks in diverse student groups. It aims to take a realistic, practical look at how teachers can encourage students to learn about, for example, engineering, history, publishing or sport science through working collaboratively in multicultural groups.

A broader view of group work issues

Ensuring that cross-cultural group work is effective starts with resolving generic issues about group work which are often wrongly labelled as arising from the students' cultural diversity. Ask most teachers or students about group work and you are more likely to hear about problems than benefits. Difficulties with group work arise from the complexity of the method itself, from students' lack of skill in working in this way but above all, from inappropriate ways in which group work is organised and assessed. For example, many teachers use groups as a way of handling ever larger numbers of students rather than as a way of enhancing students' learning. They set tasks that are actually best done individually; sometimes the groups are too large; often, teachers do not anticipate the virtually inevitable conflicts that arise and have not planned ways of dealing with problems. They tack assessment on at the end or manage it in the same way as for individual work.

Even without this kind of (mis)management, students frequently struggle to see group work as worth the effort. They often must do the work in a relatively short time and organise the project or activity around all their other demands. If they protest, teachers say that their group experience is good practice for later employment, yet students find it difficult to believe that after graduation, they will be asked to work in groups without a designated leader who has some authority to compel effort. When again, they wonder, will membership be random rather than based on having a particular expertise or role? When again will those who do not co-operate or who coast without pulling their weight suffer no consequences? If group work comprises a significant percentage of the final mark, this can provoke further tensions.

Students might tolerate these difficulties if it were not for their concern about unfair assessment. They regularly complain that marks do not reflect the value each student brings to the shared task with ineffective group members configured as a threat to final qualification or grade. This resentment can be and often is directed by one group of students at another. Home students accuse international students of 'not pulling their weight' and worry about their group's mark being 'pulled down' by the language standards of international students. International students can feel frustrated that their ideas and contributions are ignored or disregarded or that they are forced to work with home students whose motivation and diligence leaves much to be desired. Dissatisfactions are linked to language competence and disagreements arising from cross-cultural misunderstandings are interpreted as incompetence, arrogance or any number of other negative labels.

There are many sources for guidance on rethinking group work per se. You might consult the pedagogic literature, discuss the issues with experienced colleagues, and/or seek the views of institutional specialists such as educational developers. Here, the focus is on aspects that are within the teacher's remit and that are especially pertinent to multicultural group work for discipline-specific tasks. As ever, suggestions about addressing the needs of international students will also be welcomed by students who differ from their peers because they, for example, learn part time, have more experience in group tasks, and/or have a disability.

Fitting group work into the university experience

All students may need careful explanations of why a group project is a legitimate learning method but this will be especially true where the primary function is showing discipline-specific knowledge, with interaction seen as a means to that end rather than the primary focus of the group task. It will help if you are explicit about how the task links with the course objectives, and what students are expected to gain from the experience as *learners* rather than, for example, as future employees or world citizens. You may also need to explain how the method fits with the other teaching methods used in the course. However, even with the discipline-specific learning at the centre of the task, interaction is a vital component of achieving it.

How might group membership be decided?

The first expression of how willing students are to work with fellow students they see as culturally different from themselves is when establishing group membership. One frequently cited study of the reality of culturally mixed groups on Australian university campuses confirms that the large majority of students either remain within or quickly return to interactions where both parties 'feel more comfortable, think along the same wavelength, and share similar communication style and sense of humour ' (Volet and Ang, 1998, p. 10). In other words, many if not most students 'stick to their own' outside the classroom if they have the chance to do so (though, of course, every generalisation has many exceptions) and students in general but especially international students turn to fellow 'countrymen' for support, friendship and advice (UKCOSA, 2004). These patterns are usually firmly set before students arrive in your classroom though; where relationships between students are more diverse, frequent and open outside the classroom, the impact on interaction within it is probably less problematic. However, it will still be one of the factors to be considered when setting group membership.

Group membership can be set by the teacher, decided by students themselves or some combination of the two. The often-asked question, 'Which is better?' will have different answers depending on a host of factors, most of which are interrelated. The teacher's skill lies in arriving at a solution that is most likely to mean all students can achieve the learning outcomes with about the same level of challenge and effort. This ideal state can never be fully accomplished and some teachers delay a decision on this until they have had time to assess the group's interactions, but membership is a key way to establishing a more 'level playing field' for students' learning.

You may ask students to choose who is in their group if group work occurs early in the course, perhaps because you do not know them as a group or as individuals or because you decide that they need the relative safety of working within familiar rules and behaviours. Self-selection is also useful if the task is relatively short-lived and therefore not especially complex or if the assessment stresses the final product because the more diverse the group, the longer it will take to attain an end product comparable to that produced by a monocultural group (see below for more on this point). On the other hand, there are arguments against self-selection, even in the early part of a programme or for short-lived tasks. Some studies show international students prefer working in multicultural groups (Ledwith *et al.*, 1996), perhaps because it is one of the few chances they have to interact with home students and to practise using informal, discipline-specific English. Also, if later high-stakes assessment requires effective multicultural group work, then early, short-lived tasks provide practice. They may also be lower risk, in that early tasks can be judged formatively, individually or via self- or peer-assessment.

An alternative to letting students choose is for the teacher to allocate group membership. This approach is often deemed the most appropriate where the group process is being assessed, where the students are expected to develop group skills, where tasks clearly warrant a global perspective, or where the programme is committed to producing graduates with all of the above attributes. Teacher selection works best if you have some information about individual students and select membership with this in mind. Teachers with considerable experience of 'engineering' group membership suggest:

- Where international students form a relatively small proportion of the class, ensure there are at least one or two in a group rather than placing them singly in groups of home students.
- Do not assume that groups where several students share a common language (e.g. three Spanish speakers and four English speakers) will necessarily cause a split; rather, the group needs to address this issue and reach agreement about its management.
- Remain sensitive to global conflicts and recognise that students from these areas will not necessarily find it easy to work together. If you know your students, you could explore this aspect with them.
- Balance the size of the group and the relative diversity of membership; groups should never be 'too big' and five to seven is generally considered optimal, although, very diverse groups (however you define this) may need to be smaller.
- Consider using different criteria for selecting membership depending on the task. There may be times when students can allocate themselves according to their own interests with you confirming their decisions.

Creating an inclusive group work task

Group work for learning rests on assigning a task that is better done in a group than by any one person. A suitable task should involve all group members, encourage and reward use of members' skills and previous experience and, ideally, should encourage the kind of synergy that turns students' diverse skills and knowledge into an asset rather than a liability. You could do this by:

- choosing a collaborative verb when defining the task. For example, you might ask students to *compile* a catalogue of whatever is relevant to the task 'experiences, examples, images, etc.' and to *comment on* others' contribution in terms of the appropriate theories or contexts being discussed. Students might *collect* applications of a theory and *compare* their significance or *assemble* a portfolio of examples with a specific emphasis on finding diverse cases. A brief might ask students to *prepare positions* on an issue or prepare for a debate by first *documenting and justifying* a wide range of possible positions they might take. All of these tasks are better done in a group and a few can only be done that way.

- making the problem sufficiently complex so that it requires the efforts of several people. For example, you could require the group to prepare for a product launch, redesign a nearby derelict urban site or role-play a public enquiry.
- requiring students to adopt a range of stances or roles.
- asking students to identify then draw on a range of skills and abilities in the group so that, for example, a strong organiser who finds oral presentations difficult or someone with statistical skills who writes grammatically incorrect English will nevertheless be a valuable group asset. If the assessment specifically requires the group to show how and how well they used the members' diverse skills, then being different moves from being a problem to being an opportunity (a point considered further under assessment, below).
- making all students equally unsure how to proceed. 'Fuzzy' tasks (with clear task briefs) which ask all group members to explore the scope and nature of the solution or where a range of problem-solving strategies might be useful can encourage a group to put their collective heads together. Novel tasks or tasks set in unusual contexts can also be more inclusive. For example, a Business Studies lecturer found that asking students to find a solution to the problem that would work in Antarctica meant everyone started with an equally unfamiliar context.

An inclusive brief depends not just on what you ask students to do but also on what you assume about the context or about students' cultural knowledge. If such knowledge is an inherent part of the task, it must be provided. Where context knowledge or cultural knowledge is not necessary, consider excluding it. Sometimes, excluding unnecessary cultural assumptions and allusions requires little more than avoiding culturally-specific analogies (e.g. referring to a hard-to-reach group as '... the Heineken factor') or to avoiding negative stereotypes such as illustrating laziness with a drawing of a sombrero-wearing figure slumped against a wall. It is much more difficult to spot assumptions about students' general knowledge (for example, using quotations from Shakespeare or expecting students to know what someone 'as game as Ned Kelly' might be like). Students' background knowledge also needs to be explicit. If, for example, students cannot do the task unless they know how US adoption law works or what is normally included in a UK publisher's marketing plan or how land acquisition in nineteenth-century Australia contributed to the case that they are exploring, then state this requirement explicitly ('I am assuming you know about xx') and provide students who lack the background knowledge with advice about where to go to fill in their gaps.

Finally, although the learning objectives for the course will dictate what the student must do in group work, the *context* in which the task is set may be adapted to recognise all students' sensitivities. For example, one UK management course set a case study in a brewery, yet another industry would have served equally well. Choosing a brewery meant students with religious reasons to avoid alcohol had to set aside strongly held views before they could engage with the task. Of course, if you are teaching a course on managing breweries or any of a range of issues where students are likely to hold strong beliefs, then these become part of the learning outcomes. If this is not the case, considering students' sensitivities means you encourage all to be equally engaged and involved.

Assessing tasks in mixed cultural groups

An inclusive task brief encourages home and international students to value and learn from group work experiences but if you ask them to record and evaluate the way in which they achieved the task, this goes one step further. Multicultural groups will take longer to achieve the final outcome compared with monocultural ones because the group must first find ways to communicate effectively. So, unless the task lasts for many weeks, if you choose to assess only the final result, you create a situation where being diverse becomes a disadvantage. Home students in particular will take active steps to avoid such groups. Instead, assessment criteria need to both assess the learning outcomes and use methods which are equitable for all group members. If the product (i.e. what they must do) and process (i.e. how they do it) are both assessable, then you are telling students to put effort into doing both well rather than focusing on achieving a 'perfect' final artefact. Since learning is a process, you are also stressing the learning as well as encouraging home students in particular to rethink the purpose of the group's efforts.

Taking the issue of criteria first, multicultural group work is more effective if all students know what will be assessed and how marks will be allocated. If you expect students to invest energy in cross-cultural communication, in allocating roles according to students' strengths or experience, or in managing conflict effectively, then these aspects must attract a percentage of the final mark which reflects the effort involved. You must also stipulate how the students will track and record their own and others' efforts. For example, you might observe the process yourself at intervals, ask for weekly minutes of meetings, or require students to keep logs which are signed off intermittently (rather than assessed) to ensure they are contemporaneous. If students keep logs, their records can provide examples and supportive documentation for subsequent evaluation and review if you ask each student for an individual account of the group process and their learning within it.

Logging the process and requiring evidence of it can also address the central problem that many students describe when reflecting on their own group work experiences: allocating equitable marks to reflect individuals' contributions. This is problematic in all group work and even more so where multicultural membership is involved, as the last chapter describes. Generic advice on group work assessment will be useful here, especially if peer assessment is used. As the last chapter makes clear, the more diverse the group, the more effort needs to go into unpicking the tacit and implicit understandings students have of each other's

'good performance'. Criteria also need to explicitly address the relative importance of English language competence, especially in summative assessment. If
students must do a final presentation, can those who crunch the data, design the
graphs and generate the Powerpoint slides be valued equally with the person who
stands up and speaks for the group? If each person writes a section of the final
report, what will be the effect of one student's imperfect English? Will marks
reflect how the report was researched, structured, and evaluated as well as the
final draft itself? In general, both home students and international students over-
estimate the impact of English on a student's ability to contribute, though students
with low English competence will struggle with all aspects of group work, especially in the early months, and this may be a factor to take into account when
allocating group membership, especially at the start of a student's university
course.

If the teacher decides to use novel or unusual methods of assessment of group
work, these probably need rehearsal. If, for example, you decide to introduce an
oral examination or a poster presentation, will students have a chance to practise
answering questions or have a look at others' previous efforts to see what received
good marks? When students copy the model, they will need supportive formative
feedback and specific guidance on how to improve before they attempt the same
for summative assessment.

Helping the group process

Even where the task and the subject knowledge take centre stage, teachers and
students cannot overlook process issues and this is especially true where groups
are multicultural, even where the skills themselves are not assessed or specifically
taught. Teachers can model inclusive classroom behaviour and establish ground
rules that specifically target inclusivity. They might draw attention to areas where
conflict is common in multicultural groups such as how decisions are made, how
disagreements are handled, ways of encouraging others to participate, and so
on. With your help, the group could agree how they will handle these issues. In all
groups, but especially those which are very diverse, it helps to create more for-
malised structures where students adopt specific roles and perhaps rotate
responsibilities so all can see how others carry them out. Home students may be
more willing to engage with and value the contributions of international students
if the suggestions about assessment given above are adopted.

Despite all the planning, careful design of the task and sensitive use of assessment, most student groups have times when they clash rather than collaborate.
Since this is virtually inevitable, and in the case of multicultural group work,
since the differences that often cause the conflict will also mean students may not
be able to draw on shared assumptions and communication styles to resolve them,
the teacher needs to plan for intervention. You will help multicultural groups to
work more effectively if you:

- Encourage them to set ground rules for participation and discuss how they will manage conflict.
- Make clear to students what options they have when conflict arises.
- Have a stated way for addressing the issue. For example, one UK teacher draws on the way referees manage football games by using a red or yellow card to stop play. He provides students with a yellow card that they can 'play' before a given date, seeking his involvement in resolving problems.
- Observe or track group activity to spot the signs, if possible, before the situation becomes serious. In longer projects, interim tutorials provide opportunities for monitoring and collecting student feedback.

Cultures will have very different ways for manifesting and dealing with conflict so you can expect students to have a wide range of expectations and behaviours. By making explicit what you expect from them and what they can expect from you, it may be that all will learn to be more skilful in managing 'difficult moments' in a diverse group. This will never be easy but if the emphasis remains on learning from the experience and gaining useful cross-cultural communication skills, students can develop ways to use the skills in their next student group. As they will probably encounter many during their university career, it can be argued that even without being valued by assessing it per se, it is nevertheless the most useful outcome of assessed, subject-specific independent group work.

References

Ledwith, S., Lee, A., Manfredi, S. and Wildish, C. (1996). *Multiculturalism, Student Group Work and Assessment*. Oxford: Oxford Brookes University.

UKCOSA (2004) *Broadening Our Horizons: International Students in UK Universities and Colleges. UKCOSA*: The Council for International Education, London.

Volet, S. and Ang, G. (1998). 'Culturally mixed groups on international campuses: an opportunity for inter-cultural learning'. *Higher Education Research and Development*, 17, 5–23.

10

Improving teaching and learning practices for international students

Implications for curriculum, pedagogy and assessment

Dr Janette Ryan, Monash University

If international students are the 'canaries' in the coalmine as we suggest in Chapter 1, then it is necessary to examine the issues at the 'coalface' for both international students and their lecturers. This chapter focuses on the 'operational' issues and dilemmas that may surface in multicultural classrooms. It provides a summary of the problematic areas cited by international students and lecturers and provides practical suggestions as to how lecturers can improve their teaching and learning for international students in ways that will benefit all students.

Meeting students' learning needs

There is often not time in lecturers' busy lives to step back and re-assess the assumptions underpinning their practice. Student feedback instruments give lecturers some measure of the areas of their teaching which they do well and the areas that are lacking. These instruments rarely give lecturers qualitative information, however, about how they can improve their practice, in ways that are systemic and sustainable. Exhortations to 'do it better' without saying how, generally result in lecturers trying to do more to satisfy increasing demands. Lecturers need to learn how to do things differently in ways that better suit their own needs as teachers as well as the needs of the range of their students. But first lecturers need to know what areas are problematic, both for lecturers themselves and for international students.

In my own research (Ryan, 2000), asking lecturers and international students what they believed to be 'good' teaching and learning practices, both groups gave remarkably similar responses. They cited a preparedness to tailor course content, teaching methods and assessment techniques to the needs and interest of students. In many cases, the students interviewed were in the classes of the lecturers interviewed, yet the reports of how well students' needs were being met fell short of what lecturers thought they were delivering. This gap between theory and practice happened despite lecturers' dedication to meeting the needs of their students as best they could. Lecturers were often aware of what was needed but putting this into practice, that is, operationalising these ideals, was much more difficult.

The 'gap' in expectations between lecturers and international students is often the source of students' problems rather than a lack in students' own skills. Lecturers can do much to bridge this gap and so ensure that international students have better opportunities to successfully demonstrate their abilities.

'Gaps' in understanding

Many lecturers interviewed held misconceptions about international students which have already been reviewed elsewhere in this book. My studies confirmed that teachers sometimes viewed international students as a homogeneous group with similar learning styles and expectations; as rote learners with a surface approach to learning; as unwilling to participate in class discussion; and as only wanting to interact with others from similar backgrounds. International students reported that they felt under-valued and misunderstood. They wanted to learn new skills, to demonstrate their experience and expertise, and to speak up and participate in class, but needed help to do so. My interviews showed that international students liked doing group work and using independent and critical approaches to learning. They needed lecturers to assist them by employing a range of strategies such as providing background knowledge; avoiding the use of slang and not speaking too fast; referring to international or multicultural as well as local examples; and by providing opportunities to work and mix with home students.

There were many examples where lecturers were making genuine attempts to improve their practice, generally through a trial-and-error process. Many found that one solution worked for one group of students in a given year but needed to be changed and adapted to the following cohort of students. That is, lecturers found that there are differences in the curriculum as 'intention' (as stated in course objectives and outcomes) and curriculum as 'outcome' (as evidenced by what the students had actually learnt and experienced). Lecturers who understood the nexus between these two were generally those who understood the need to be flexible and reflective practitioners. They understood that teaching and learning are dynamic parts of a whole and that they could learn as much from their students as students could from them. They appreciated that the interaction between teachers and learners determines and shapes educational outcomes. They were comfortable with the co-construction of knowledge and learning, with different approaches and strategies despite there often being variable success. The types of learning tasks and materials that they provided were designed to facilitate a broad range of learning styles and interests that could be negotiated and adapted to suit a diverse range of students. They provided for this diversity not just in classroom activities but in the whole range of teaching and learning activities – in the curriculum (materials), pedagogy (teaching methods) and assessment (judgements of outcomes). Students in these classes reported an increased sense of ownership of their learning and of respect for them as independent learners. This, of course, was of benefit to all students within the classroom but of particular importance for international students who may often have difficulty negotiating a sometimes very unfamiliar learning environment.

Although problematic areas for international students can vary according to discipline area, there are some key generic issues in curriculum content, pedagogy and assessment where lecturers can improve their teaching and learning practices in ways that will not only benefit international students, but all students.

Curriculum content and design

'Internationalisation' of curriculum content and design is dealt with in some detail in Chapters 12 and 13, which make clear that internationalisation goes beyond the mere addition of international examples. It needs to permeate the very nature of the discipline so that students gain a global understanding and perspective of the discipline. Both curriculum content and design need to foster both international and local perspectives of the discipline. It is not just a matter of adjusting, or 'adding' to curriculum content to ensure that it suits international students, but making sure that home students also gain global and international understandings. Two specific aspects of the curriculum, however, are highlighted here.

Reference/reading lists

Copious amounts of reading present problems for many international students (see Chapter 6) as it can take them huge amounts of time to translate the information, or to understand the background content of the materials. There are many ways that lecturers can assist international students to access relevant information more easily, such as:

- the selective use of references/readings
- providing annotated bibliographies
- marking key texts
- identifying relevant chapters or excerpts
- using electronic materials (for faster searching of relevant information)
- checking the accessibility of texts or websites used (for Plain English and straightforward and pertinent information)
- checking the relevance of the language used and making sure it is appropriate for the target audience
- including foundational or definitive texts
- providing reading lists early
- making unit or module descriptions available electronically
- providing a glossary of key terms and concepts.

Placements/field work

Field work and field placements provide opportunities for students to expand their perspectives, especially in areas where lecturers themselves may have little knowledge or experience. It can therefore be useful, especially in practice-based courses, to provide students with opportunities for:

- a placement outside the local region
- diverse placements/field trips within the local region
- opportunities for national or international placements or work.

Pedagogy

Teaching practices provide opportunities for the development of globally orientated knowledge and intercultural understandings and skills for all students, as well as for catering for the learning needs of international students. International students need to be given opportunities to be able to participate and demonstrate their skills, and equally home students need to learn how to listen to and learn from the experiences of others. In this way, international students become an important source of expertise for home students. In order to do this, lecturers also need to examine fundamental issues about their teaching and learning practices. These include questions such as:

- Do you provide a supportive learning environment where all students are able to participate successfully and demonstrate their abilities?
- Do you engage students in learning, drawing on their experiences and interests?
- Are you a critically reflective practitioner? Can you identify the assumptions underpinning your teaching and learning practices? Do you examine these to ensure that outcomes for students are equitable?

Creating supportive learning environments

Lecturers need to create the contexts where students feel that their contributions are valued and that they are given opportunities to participate and succeed. Lecturers need to:

- provide a range of opportunities for all students to demonstrate their abilities, such as through choice of assessment or group discussion topics or class activities;
- provide negotiable class discussions and assessment tasks and methods so that students can explore their own areas of interest and demonstrate their knowledge and expertise;
- examine whether learning objectives can be met in other, more inclusive, ways such as through different tasks, formats or methods, or in different time frames;
- facilitate contact between home students and students from other cultures through organising and facilitating multicultural group work and discussion (see Chapters 8 and 9).

Engaging students in learning

Lecturers need to ensure that international students can draw upon their background knowledge and experience in order to make the connections with and foundations for their new knowledge and understandings. Providing opportunities for students to express and discuss their views in tutorials or seminars is not easy but lecturers encourage this if they:

- experiment with a variety of approaches to encourage students' participation, such as giving them time to formulate responses or engineering small group composition differently;
- frequently check students' understandings as to unit content and assessment task requirements;
- draw on the diverse background experiences and knowledge of students to enrich the learning environment for all students.

Being a critically reflective teacher

Lecturers need to re-examine their own practices to ensure that they are relevant to the needs of international students and provide equitable outcomes. For lecturers, this means:

- being aware of the cultural underpinnings of their own teaching and learning practices;
- examining whether their teaching either advantages or disadvantages different groups of students;
- evaluating unit or module requirements, including unit content, materials, classroom practices, assessment tasks and student learning outcomes, to ensure that there are no barriers to students' participation and success;
- thinking about whether any class or assessment tasks may cause difficulties for any group of students (e.g. due to ethnic background, religious beliefs, gender).

Lecture design and delivery

The areas that international students find most problematic relate to lectures (i.e. understanding lecture content) and tutorials or seminars (i.e. being able to participate). The conventional lecture format can present many problems for international students, as described in Chapter 6. This is especially true when lectures include large amounts of information and assume certain background knowledge and language proficiency. Making minor changes to the style of presentation can assist many students to more effectively understand the content and concepts contained in the lecture. This can include:

- providing a framework for each lecture, stating its main objectives, and how it links to previous and future topics;
- summarising the main points of the lecture;
- 'flagging' important information through the use of phrases such as 'this is a key point';
- pausing after key information or repeating or re-phrasing the information to allow more time for note taking;
- speaking clearly, using Plain English, and clarifying any new or unfamiliar vocabulary or concepts, then spelling them out or writing them down;
- speaking a little more slowly, especially when key information is being covered;
- providing lecture notes in advance or via the web;
- providing a 'question box' where students can leave questions after the lecture which can be addressed in tutorials or in the following lecture.

Encouraging participation in tutorials and seminars

In tutorials, international students need to be given opportunities to participate and demonstrate their knowledge and abilities. This can mean encouraging students to talk about their own experiences and ensuring that these become part of the class discussion. Often international students want to contribute but might not yet have the language facility or be familiar with the appropriate cultural mores for participation. This may mean that the tutor needs to give international students adequate time to prepare their responses and be sensitive to different ways of responding. The tutor also needs to be sensitive to students' different approaches to knowledge and learning and ensure that these are given equal 'space' and respect in the classroom. The tutor can do much to model a 'tone' of acceptance and nurturing of diversity, even displaying their own learning from unfamiliar perspectives.

The most problematic area for international students is often group discussions as they may lack background information or language proficiency, and the tutor needs to engineer and monitor these discussions to ensure that all students learn to value others' contributions. The use of ground rules for participation can be very effective, especially if they explicitly cover both group processes as well as group product, and stipulate task allocation and roles, turn-taking in discussions, conflict management, identification of groups members' strengths and weaknesses, and how group diversity has been productively used.

Tutors can feel uncomfortable when their questions in tutorials are met with silence and they can rush to fill the gap, often gratefully letting more vocal local students dominate the discussion. Sometimes students perceive that tutors are playing a 'fishing' game where the tutor responds positively to the answer they are looking for and this can prevent students from taking risks. Most students (but not all) learn to play the 'game' and can display their knowledge more easily. It can be uncomfortable when students do not respond in class in the ways that tutors normally expect, and this can sometimes be communicated negatively to students. If tutors do not respond to the contributions made by international students, because they are difficult to understand or are unfamiliar, the tutor's body language or facial expression can sometimes betray a lack of understanding or acceptance. It is important that tutors take the time to try to understand what a student has said, even if this can take some effort at understanding and perhaps follow-up questions, and to try to 'translate' it for the class and ensure that it becomes part of the discussion. All students need to feel that they are accepted as full members of the class.

International students report that they do want to participate but they often don't know how, lack the language facility to express their opinion or any sophistication of thought, and that it takes much courage to make a verbal contribution when they know that their language is clumsy and that they may not have understood. Many international students report that it can take them at least six months to summon the courage to speak in class, and if they receive a negative response, it can take much longer to muster the confidence to make another attempt. Many lecturers underestimate the abilities of international students, especially in the early stages of their study when they may be struggling with mastering the language. International students are aware that they sound clumsy and even 'stupid'. This can make it difficult for them to work in groups and even to make friends. Sheer fear of embarrassment prevents them from participating.

Tutors may often ask international students if they understand and students will say 'yes' when it is clear that they do not. When placed in such a situation, international students may feel too embarrassed to repeatedly admit that they don't understand and may not want to hold the class back. They prefer to say 'yes' to avoid the uncomfortable attention. Many students (including home students) prefer to remain silent in class. The tutor cannot force participation but can act to ensure that there are ample opportunities for participation and that students feel safe and supported when they choose to participate. Some possible strategies for doing this include:

- jointly developing with students 'ground rules' for whole group and small group discussion and participation;
- modelling inclusive speaking and listening practices by taking time to understand international students' contributions and, if necessary, 'translating' them in a diplomatic way for the rest of the class;
- ensuring that international students' contributions become part of the class discussion, even if this takes the discussion in a different direction;
- giving students time to formulate their responses to questions (through early provision of questions or through small group or pair work);
- engineering the composition of groups (for example, through allowing students to choose one friend to work with and then pairing them into groups of four that are diverse);
- structuring group tasks so that diversity of skills and knowledge is required and rewarded;

- showing an interest in students' background knowledge and experiences (but don't expect them to talk on behalf of their culture);
- providing some time in class for one-on-one conversations and for checking of progress and understanding of the tasks.

Assessment

The evaluation and grading of student work is a contentious area for most students, but international students will often have the most difficulty in decoding lecturers' expectations. They may also have reduced opportunities for demonstrating their learning and knowledge. Lecturers need to recognise that what they consider to be academic ability can be culturally based. They may reward for facility with academic discourse rather than what students have actually learnt or the depth of their understanding. They need to ensure that their assessment techniques match the learning objectives. Lecturers need to ask themselves:

- Are they assessing students for their mastery of academic discourse rather than for their critical or original thinking?
- Do they recognise or encourage different styles and approaches to learning?
- Do they allow students to use their own words and ways of expressing themselves?
- Do they assess content rather than penalise for spelling or grammatical expression except in the cases where spelling and grammar are inherent in the assessment criteria?

Many assessment tasks, especially essays, contain hidden codes or 'prompts' only apparent to students familiar with the academic discourse. For example, an essay topic that comprises a controversial statement followed by the word 'Discuss' may not signal to an international student that they are expected to challenge the statement, and that the essay should contain the student's own evaluation and opinion. The ways that international students write might also reflect different views about the nature and ownership of knowledge. It is therefore imperative for all students that expected paradigms and conventions are clearly articulated and modelled so that accusations of plagiarism, for example, can be avoided. Many international students can find themselves being punished for behaviour that was previously rewarded. In such cases it is important to take an educative approach to plagiarism and syndication (shared work) rather than simply a punitive one. It is also important that international students receive early feedback and encouragement. Such comments need to be descriptive, indicating what has been done well and what needs to be done in order to improve. It can also be helpful to model appropriate responses in class or to provide exemplars of previous successful work.

Anyone reviewing their own assessment methods and tasks could include questions such as:

- Are requirements and expectations explicit?
- Are there hidden codes or 'prompts'?
- Do the assessment tasks match the learning objectives?
- Do assessment tasks allow for different ways of demonstrating achievement of the learning objectives?
- Are students being assessed on what they have learnt or what they already know?
- Are content and understanding, or style and facility with language being assessed?
- If facility with language is important, are you teaching this skill?
- Is there a choice of topics so that students can connect with their own background knowledge and experiences?
- Can students work on topics that are relevant to their backgrounds and futures?
- Are assessment tasks flexible and negotiable?
- Is there a range of modes of presentation e.g. written, oral, 'hands on'?
- Is there a mixture of individual and group tasks?
- Can students choose the weighting of the task within a range so that they can take advantage of their strengths?
- Are tasks self-directed?
- Can assessment topics be provided that are less parochial and more internationalised?
- Can opportunities for plagiarism be 'designed out' by the choice of assessment task and topic?

Conclusion

By re-examining their teaching and learning practices, lecturers can make changes that are more sustainable for them as teachers and more suitable for the diverse range of students, not just international students. The use of 'internationalised' pedagogy means that all students not only gain more globalised knowledge but also develop the skills and attitudes to work in global settings. This requires that the teacher also has some level of global knowledge, skills and attitudes and a willingness to create spaces for all students with full rights of participation and success. Such a broad worldview can underpin teaching and learning philosophies but may only require minor adjustments to teaching and learning practices as the teacher becomes a more active facilitator of learning rather than the bastion of conventional wisdom.

References

Ryan, J. (2000). *A Guide to Teaching International Students*. Oxford: Oxford Centre for Staff and Learning Development.

11

Postgraduate supervision

Dr Janette Ryan, Monash University

This chapter is adapted with permission from *A Guide to Teaching International Students* (2000) published by the Oxford Centre for Staff and Learning Development, Oxford Brookes University.

Relationship and boundaries

In the same way as for undergraduate students, international postgraduate students will be shaped by their previous educational experiences and expectations. They are likely to expect a hierarchical relationship with their supervisor where the supervisor exercises tight control over the research. Many international students will expect their supervisor to take the initiative and adopt a role close to being a guide and/or parent. They may expect their supervisor to make major contributions toward the research and the thesis. They will be expecting clear direction and guidance from their supervisors, whom they will hold in high esteem, and they will often have very high expectations of the relationship. They usually assume the supervisor is very knowledgeable in their area of study.

Many will be totally unprepared for the independence and isolation of postgraduate study. They may be unfamiliar with the extending and speculative approach expected of postgraduate students and the expectations of the creation of 'new knowledge' may be culturally foreign to them. They may have no experience of literature searching, critical reading, or specialised research skills. They may be lacking in library, computer, and laboratory skills. Home students, too, may feel the same sense of surprise and disappointment but may have many more skills and strategies for adapting and negotiating a suitable relationship with supervisors.

On taught courses, international students complain of too little structure and too little control exercised by staff. On research-only courses, international students will often only have their supervisor to relate to, and the relationship therefore becomes paramount. The first six months are crucial, and this is the time when the relationship needs to be clearly negotiated and understood.

The relationship between student and supervisor will be further complicated by the fact that there are no explicit rules for supervision of postgraduate students.

These are often developed as a result of the supervisor's own experience of supervision, information derived from broad guidelines produced by the institution, or may be simply based on tradition. For students who have come from education systems where student-teacher relationships are hierarchical and clearly defined, international postgraduates may be bewildered by the lack of clarity in their new relationship with their supervisor and some may seek to establish relationships closer to what they are expecting to find.

The supervisor's view

The relationship can be a difficult one for supervisors as well. Supervisors report that international students require a considerable amount of their time and energy and that a lot of this time is taken filling in gaps in students' background knowledge, and in their practical experiences.

Many international students feel that it is important that their supervisors have some knowledge of their (the student's) home country and understanding of their culture. The importance of an empathetic relationship between student and supervisor is illustrated by the story of a Chinese postgraduate student in Australia, quoted in Ryan and Zuber-Skerritt (1999). The student explained her experiences in finding a new, sympathetic supervisor after having a poor experience with an unsympathetic one:

> He taught me how to adjust my thinking to accommodate Western ways – together we built a bridge that I could cross ... Everything I said, he understood ... I laugh – he laughed. He very much understands the ways of the Chinese student. He went to teach in China and he understands the Chinese culture and educational system. He is able to understand the Chinese students and the difficulties we face here. He also understands why I have come here ... He would ask me what it was that I was thinking about in my writing. I would just know the main ideas and he would help me find the hidden meanings in the books that I am reading. One paragraph at a time he would explain things and show me the argument that he would make. I soon learned that making this argument was not easy but as I changed my ways, I could do it, too. He showed me how to do this. He knew that I was not stupid because he understood the Chinese ways. I have never thought this way before and I am learning that it is a good way to think. At the moment I am not perfect but I am getting better.
>
> (33–4)

Problems in the relationship

Postgraduate international students can experience enormous difficulties, particularly if there are misunderstandings with their supervisors. They can start to withdraw and become very isolated, and some go into a downward spiral. They then need a 'lifeline' of some kind to bring them back on track. One international postgraduate student retreated into the postgraduate study room, and began virtually living there. He was eventually befriended by a cleaner, who gave him items he needed to survive, and this was the only thing that prevented him from giving up his studies and returning home. Another became completely isolated in his faculty to the point where he had contact with no one and the staff were completely unaware of the work he was doing in the laboratory. He complained of racial discrimination by other members of staff and was ostracised. Eventually, another member of the teaching staff befriended him, asked about his background and his country, and took an interest in his work. It became clear that there had been a misunderstanding between him and his supervisor that had led to the situation arising. After this, he was able to continue his work successfully. Such problems can be avoided by early clarification of roles and expectations of the relationship. If you allocate supervisors:

- Try to ensure a good and productive match of student and supervisor; look for mutual knowledge and respect.
- Try to allocate supervisors with overseas experience, cultural sensitivity or intercultural communication skills, empathy, or who have background knowledge of the student's home country or culture.

If you are a supervisor:

- Clarify roles of both student and supervisor early.
- Discuss expectations on both sides to avoid future misunderstandings.
- Set boundaries and limits to what you are prepared to do.
- Schedule regular appointments which both parties are responsible for keeping.
- Record decisions made during meetings.
- Provide more assistance early and gradually assist the student to develop more independent learning approaches.
- Try to assess where your student is academically; assess their knowledge of the discipline.

Recognise added pressures

Although international students may be undergoing enormous cultural changes and stress, it may be difficult for some students to express dissatisfaction of criticism. You may have to try hard to 'read between the lines'. International students may have different ways of expressing needs and difficulties than you are expecting. Your international students will have to work much harder compared with home students, especially in the time needed for background reading. You will help in this area if you assist students in identifying key texts and authors so that they do not waste valuable reading time on those that are not useful. You could suggest advice on general texts that fill in gaps in background knowledge or identify a small number of key texts or articles for the student to read at the beginning of their studies.

Provide practical advice

Many students but especially international students will lack background knowledge in the subject area. You could assist them to identify key current debates within their area of study or alert them to conferences or other scholars with whom they should make contact. Facilitating their contact with other students for learning and for social support will be helpful. Finally, you will need to regularly check that the student is making progress.

Improving research skills

Supervisors commonly assume too much of students' research knowledge. Some international students will have very little knowledge of how to conduct research and will need considerable guidance in the early stages. They may welcome training in a range of skills such as advanced research methods, computer skills, literacy skills, and assistance in how to find sources and materials. They often also need to be gradually introduced to the academic discourse of the discipline so that they can start to become active members.

You may find your international students lack practical experiences or discover their competence in these areas needs to be investigated. They may have previously learned in a text-based way, rather than through activity-based learning. In the sciences, they may lack laboratory experience and may need assistance with laboratory practices and protocols. Students who have little laboratory experience or who have worked in laboratories that were less well equipped, or with less technically advanced equipment, may need more training and help from demonstrators and technicians. They may also need help with reading technical instructions and manuals. Working on practical tasks in small groups with other students can be an excellent tool for international students in facilitating interaction and improving their language and communication skills.

As with laboratories, some international students may have fewer or less advanced computer skills and will need extra assistance. Clear instructions and information given in small 'chunks' will help and ensure new learning is reinforced by frequent practice. Of course, some come from educational systems where exactly the opposite is the case – they have had more access to information, technology and research skills than are on offer in their new situation. But where you spot a gap, it will help to organise training in special skills.

If you are planning for specialised training, this could be informal, perhaps by placing international students in groups with students who already have good laboratory skills and knowledge. Formal instruction may be more appropriate where safety is paramount or where universities provide targeted programmes for international postgraduates. To check instructions have been understood, ask students to do a 'dry run' of the procedures first before using the actual equipment.

Postgraduate writing

Many international postgraduate students will have had very little experience in any kind of extended writing, and may have previously only been required to take lecture notes. (See Chapter 7 for more general guidance on developing students writing.) They may therefore resort to an oral style or may use writing styles that are favoured in their own countries. The use of proverbs, stories and literary allusions, for example, are commonly used in Asian and African writing to demonstrate one's educational level and accomplishment, and to win the reader over to the author's point of view. Such devices establish credibility and empathy. Classical sayings or poetic phrases make the writing look 'well educated'. The writing process takes a more circuitous approach, where the reader is gradually taken along a journey and the argument or main thesis only appears at the very end. The thesis begins by describing what the topic is not before describing what it is.

To help students who write using the devices described above, you could:

- Ask for written work early, discussing content and layout but avoiding editing or rewriting work at this stage.
- Encourage international postgraduates to look at previous theses; use them to discuss different approaches and structures; ask students to discuss these theses critically.
- Suggest students keep a learning journal and compile a glossary of new words, terms and concepts.
- Show how to use sources appropriately, mindful of the risk of plagiarising and demonstrating paraphrase and synthesis.

Communication

Finally, good communication between the supervisor and the student are vital for the continuing health of the relationship, and to ensure that international postgraduate students do not become isolated and disconnected. It is also a good idea to encourage your students to participate in research seminars and postgraduate student associations that can provide emotional and social support as well as opportunities for discussion and sharing amongst students with similar research interests. A broad network amongst other staff and students will increase the support systems for postgraduate students in the often lonely pursuit of postgraduate study.

References

Ryan, Y. & Zuber-Skerritt, O. (eds). (1999). *Supervising Postgraduates from Non-English Speaking Backgrounds* (pp. 40–47). Buckingham: The Society for Research into Higher Education and Open University Press.

Part III

Internationalising the curriculum

12

Internationalisation of curriculum

An institutional approach

Professor Graham Webb, Monash University

Introduction

This chapter outlines ways of developing an institutional approach to internationalisation of curriculum. The development of curriculum to take account of internationalisation has been driven, for the most part, by teachers 'at the chalk-face' confronting a variety of issues. Such issues have been occasioned by universities expanding their 'on-shore' international student numbers, by expansion to offshore campuses and partnership arrangements, by the growing diversity of the domestic student cohort and by the general desire to have curriculum keep pace with the issues and concerns provoked by internationalisation. At some point, therefore, universities as institutions have come to realise that an overall approach to internationalisation of the curriculum may be desirable in guiding the efforts of staff confronting such issues in the everyday context of the classroom.

Rationale for internationalisation of curriculum

The need to explain why internationalisation of the curriculum is an important issue, and an especially important one for an organisation such as a university, is a primary requirement that needs to be in place prior to the systematic development of strategies. Academics generally require compelling reason and argument before accepting any institutional strategy. So too do students, and articulating a compelling reason for the development of students who will be better equipped to face the modern world is another aspect of the rationale for internationalisation.

The responsibility for development of the concept of internationalisation of the curriculum may be placed in the hands of a working party or similar group with both representation (to ensure widespread ownership of the work) and expert input. In developing the concept it may be pointed out that universities are an integral part of the world economy and the world's social and political infrastructure. They have historically contributed to international understanding and collaboration and have often provided local sites for tolerance and acceptance of the unfamiliar and novel. It is therefore natural that as global forces such as the spread of multinational companies and the development of information technology impact on world systems, there are consequences for universities, and the curriculum of universities. Universities are also in a unique position to influence future directions as they help to develop the people who will make critical decisions for the future.

As part of their preparation to live and work in a globalising world, graduates need increasingly well-developed lifelong learning skills and attitudes, including an international perspective. They need to be knowledgeable about and open to views that differ from their own. They need to interpret local problems within a wider and more global framework and to judge the importance of global phenomena for their own lives and work. Internationalisation of the curriculum therefore incorporates a range of values, including openness, tolerance and culturally inclusive behaviour, which are necessary to ensure that cultural differences are heard and explored.

Graduates are encouraged to develop by the opportunities they receive through the university curriculum they experience. As curriculum refers to both the content (knowledge, skills and attitudes) and the process of teaching and learning, internationalisation of the curriculum must consider both 'what is taught/what is learned' and 'how it is taught/how it is learned'.

Developing a concept for internationalisation of curriculum

In developing a concept for internationalisation of the curriculum, it is important to acknowledge that the curriculum never stands still. As the curriculum continues to develop international dimensions, there is a need for new thinking and new methods, for change and innovation. Change occurs as the curriculum is reinterpreted and developed in light of local needs and understandings: by engagement with the local. Starting from the local understanding of students is a truism of adult learning theory and student-centredness expects the construction and challenge of new knowledge to develop from what is already known.

However, engagement with local contexts and processes increasingly raises the issue of how these relate to the wider context and to the major, global issues that are shaping the world. Opening the curriculum to internationalisation is therefore firstly about opening teaching and learning to change, to finding innovative ways of changing and adapting, to contextualising local engagement within a wider frame of reference and to understanding the local implications of global phenomena. In short, to act locally it is necessary to understand the global.

Similarly, the global is understood and interpreted effectively by reference to local experience, scholarship and research. The concept of a *relational* view sees internationalisation as a fundamental aspect of curriculum change and development, rather than an 'add-on'. It also goes further than particular manifestations of curriculum change, such as the incorporation of international examples or comparisons into a standard Australian or British curriculum. Although such approaches may be extremely useful, they need to be interpreted within the wider relational view of internationalisation of curriculum: in themselves they do not represent a comprehensive response. The idea of internationalisation of curriculum is more radical and refers to the integration of a global perspective to curriculum development. This means that content does not arise out of a single cultural base but engages with global plurality in terms of sources of knowledge. It encourages students to explore how knowledge is produced, distributed and utilised globally. It helps students develop an understanding of the global nature of scientific, technological, economic, political and cultural exchange. A relational view, such as this, is one example of an institutional conceptualisation of the issue.

Definitions of internationalisation of curriculum

The term 'globalisation' is often used to denote major forces affecting the world (such as the development of information technology) while 'internationalisation' often refers to the playing out of such forces in the specific contexts of nation states. However, there is considerable opportunity for slippage and for common or alternative use. Knight and de Wit (1995) suggest that there is no standard definition of internationalisation. In fact, definitions of internationalisation abound, including the following:

> Internationalisation is a process that prepares the community for successful participation in an increasingly interdependent world . . . The process should infuse all facets of the post-secondary education system, fostering global understanding and developing skills for effective living and working in a diverse world.
>
> (Francis, 1993)

> Internationalisation can be characterised as a process of transformation in which areas of activity are increasingly geared to operating in international surroundings, under international market conditions and with an international professional orientation.
>
> (Haarlov, 1997)

> Internationalisation of higher education is the process of integrating an international/intercultural dimension into the teaching, research and service of the institution.
>
> (Knight cited in IDP, 1996)

Such definitions may be augmented descriptively, as illustrated in the following example:

> Internationalisation includes teachers and students learning from each other, meeting the needs of overseas, offshore and local students, creating interdependence between students, viewing our professional practice from diverse

perspectives, using culturally inclusive teaching practices, accessing teaching and learning resources which reflect diversity, and offering high quality courses which are internationally relevant. Internationalisation is not merely a matter of recruiting international students, though the presence of international students is an enormous resource for the university. The aim of internationalisation is to produce graduates capable of solving problems in a variety of locations with cultural and environmental sensitivity.

(Aulakh *et al.*, 1997)

Van der Wende's (1996) typology of internationalisation for the OECD has been influential in this area, with nine characteristics of international curricula being classified as:

1   curricula with international content;
2   curricula that add a comparative dimension to traditional content;
3   career-oriented curricula;
4   curricula addressing cross-cultural skills;
5   interdisciplinary area study programmes;
6   curricula leading to internationally recognised professions;
7   curricula leading to joint or double degrees;
8   curricula whose parts are offered at off-shore institutions by local faculty;
9   special curricula designed exclusively for foreign students.

These definitions, descriptions and typology illustrate the possibilities for a university in moving towards its own definition of internationalisation generally and internationalisation of curriculum in particular.

Before moving on to consider some strategies for 'normalising' internationalisation of curriculum within university operations, it may be useful to consider the context within which the need for 'normalisation' has developed. A number of phases marking the development of different pressures and contexts for internationalisation of curriculum are suggested below.

Phases in internationalisation of curriculum

International students studying alongside home students

A major factor in the development of internationalisation of curriculum at many universities in countries such as Australia and the United Kingdom has been the influx of international students to local campuses. This has created great opportunities for development, as well as serious problems. There has always been rhetoric encouraging all students to engage in the content and teaching processes of the curriculum, and whether or not the rhetoric was actually delivered, certainly teaching to fewer students than is currently the case and who tended to come from a relatively privileged and homogenous educational background, posed fewer problems concerning student engagement. 'Massification' presented real challenges to the rhetoric of engagement. In Australia and the United Kingdom, international student numbers increased dramatically over a short period, forming far more diverse student cohorts which included older students, often with family responsibilities, working part-time and coming from less privileged educational backgrounds. However, to some extent diversity was still masked by a shared language and culture.

Although international students have been present in many Australian and United Kingdom universities for many years, the major increase in numbers has been unprecedented, with international students now comprising more than 20 per cent of the student cohort in many universities. With increasing pressure from massification and with fee paying becoming important in international student recruitment, problems that need to be faced in making the curriculum relevant and engaging for a diverse student body were brought to the fore. No longer could a common culture and understanding be assumed, but there were sometimes language problems too, meaning that the medium for solving problems could itself be problematic. So despite many Australian and United Kingdom universities having enjoyed a relatively large cohort of international students for many years, the first major phase of internationalisation of the curriculum may still be seen as the attempt by universities to cope with the more recent influx of international students and the need to ensure that they received support in order to arrive, survive and cope with life in their new learning environment. This first phase of 'survival' was also mirrored in the curriculum.

Without significantly changing the curriculum, the first modern phase of internationalisation included attempts to ensure the survival of international students by whatever methods could be found to work. These included staff taking more time to go over the curriculum with individuals and groups, encouraging the formation of self-help groups (especially for students coming from traditions of group-based learning) and the early identification of language or learning problems (e.g. making more explicit the expectations for writing a scientific report or essay, or coaching in study skills, etc.). Problems were seen to be at an individual or particular group level and solutions were similarly found by specific individuals or specific members of support groups.

Systematic curriculum development for internationalisation

A second phase of internationalisation of curriculum may be seen as a change in emphasis from survival measures developed by individuals to the more systematic development of curriculum. Not content to make up for perceived 'deficiencies' in the adjustment of international students to a standard curriculum, there was a move to develop the curriculum in order to take greater account of diversity. The starting point for this has sometimes been an audit of internationalisation of curriculum with a view to finding out what is actually happening and to bringing forward innovative or 'good practice' examples. At a basic level this may entail the identification and explanation of words, examples or experiences that mystify international students. It may also include more explanation and checking for understanding of examples or cases, with more effort placed on making explicit the initial understanding necessary to interpret the curriculum, rather than simply taking this for granted. Development of the curriculum may also see the use of more international examples, or materials or comparisons. For example, it has long been the case that the curriculum has thrived on textbooks from other countries. Now, with Internet linkages so easily embedded, curriculum materials are increasingly influenced by international materials. Of course, with the ease of gaining international information comes the associated risk posed by media domination and cultural imperialism – which also offer productive areas for curriculum and student discourse.

Transnational operations and internationalisation of curriculum

Although beyond the scope of this book, it should be noted that Australian and United Kingdom universities have developed campuses, centres and partnership agreements in many countries beyond their own borders. There are some issues in this, as one of the strong reasons drawing students to take courses offered by Australian and United Kingdom universities abroad is the name of the university and the prestige of an Australian or United Kingdom award. There is a tension between the wishes of these students for the standards and content of the provider country and the need for relevance within their own context. There is a similar tension between wishing to keep control of the curriculum from the provider country and the need to have the staff who are employed abroad own and contribute to the development of the curriculum. It is unlikely that there is one solution to internationalisation of curriculum that will apply to all types of transnational operation but in general, the stronger the relationship and understanding that is developed between the provider country and transnational operations, the better will be the outcome for the curriculum, students and teachers.

Normalising internationalisation of curriculum

A fourth phase of internationalisation of the curriculum would see the normalisation or integration of internationalisation incorporated into the normal structures, operations and practices of universities. In the area of teaching and learning, for example, it may be that the university has policy and strategy to develop student-centred and flexible learning, student rights and responsibilities, teachers' skills in terms of working with students, modelling scholarly values, encouraging cooperation and active learning, providing prompt and helpful feedback, and respecting diversity by demonstrating inclusiveness and care. These issues for teaching and learning know no boundaries and are also reinterpreted with each new technology that teachers utilise in order to assist students to learn and develop. The point is that in each of these areas, and others, internationalisation needs to become an expected and normal consideration. In the following section, a number of strategies to support 'normalisation' of internationalisation of curriculum, mainly at institutional level, are outlined.

Strategies for normalising internationalisation of curriculum

In order to realise the view of internationalisation of curriculum developed thus far, many strategies and initiatives may be advanced. The following are strategies that are sufficiently general, and sufficiently important, that they should apply to any university.

(i) Rationale and conceptualisation

The university has developed a clear written conceptualisation and rationale for internationalisation generally and internationalisation of curriculum as a subset of this. The conceptualisation follows from the university's statements of its values and purposes and its reasons for internationalisation.

(ii) Definition

The university has adopted a clear definition of both internationalisation and internationalisation of curriculum.

(iii) Planning documents

Internationalisation of curriculum is identified in all relevant university plans; for example, the university strategic plan, learning and teaching plan, support services plan, research plan, staff development plan, campus plans, faculty plans, school and departmental plans.

(iv) Approval

The need to address internationalisation of curriculum is a requirement identified in the forms and process for each new unit (subject) and course approval.

(v) Monitoring

Monitoring of units and courses, usually in the form of student and peer evaluations, includes consideration of internationalisation of curriculum. Other monitoring devices may include consideration of unit-based attrition and completion data, institutional and course level surveys, graduate destination data, employer and other stakeholder surveys and student exit surveys. All may reveal information concerning the success of strategies to internationalise curricula.

(vi) Review

The need to address internationalisation of the curriculum is a requirement for all academic reviews including course, department, school and faculty reviews. The data gained from monitoring activity is often a key aspect of internal self-review prior to the development of documentation for the external aspect of review.

(vii) Graduate attributes

Knowledge, skills and attitudes concerning internationalisation are identified in the university's statement and development of graduate attributes.

(viii) Staffing profile

There is an institutional commitment to develop a staffing profile that reflects diversity and the need to improve recruitment from minority groups. It is important that students actually experience internationalisation in terms of interacting with staff from diverse backgrounds.

(ix) Student profile and distribution

There is an institutional plan for the student profile to ensure not only a diverse student cohort, but also that there is a good distribution of diversity across discipline areas and campuses, in order to avoid 'ghettos' of students from particular backgrounds over-populating particular courses or campuses.

(x) Performance Management

The development of internationalisation of the curriculum is referred to in the performance management process (e.g. appraisal) with teaching staff being asked to comment on how they have developed internationalisation of curricula that they teach (review) and their plans for further development over the year ahead (future engagement profile).

(xi) Reward

There is recognition for achievements in developing internationalisation of curriculum as, for example, in university or faculty level awards for such achievements. Teaching development grant schemes at university or faculty level support internationalisation of curriculum as a priority area for allocation of funding. Internal research grant schemes support internationalisation that leads to strengthening of the teaching–research nexus with regard to internationalisation.

(xii) Recruitment, induction, probation and promotion

Achievements in internationalisation of the curriculum are recognised in the recruitment of new staff and in their induction to the organisation. Internationalisation of curriculum is also an area for consideration during probation, and achievement in this area is assessed prior to confirmation of appointment, and within the documentation and processes used for promotion.

(xiii) Organisational and staff development

There is an organisational and staff development plan identifying internationalisation of the curriculum as a priority area. For example, organisational development may include important university committees dedicating a meeting to participation in a workshop concerning internationalisation of curriculum. This may also be considered in the induction of new leaders and in leadership development programmes. Outside experts may inform such occasions and also participate in staff development activities. The staff development effort (e.g. individual consultations, workshops, the development of on-line materials, etc.) supports internationalisation of curriculum as an identified priority.

(xiv) Internal and external communications

Internal communication may include dissemination of 'good practice' in this area at department/school, faculty and university level, via relevant publications and websites. Faculties may organise workshops or mini conferences to communicate and celebrate achievements in the area. External communications requires university and faculty level publicity and marketing to target the importance of internationalisation of curriculum and to disseminate successes in this area when communicating with external groups such as potential students, alumni, employers, professional associations, etc.

Conclusion

By addressing each of the areas outlined above, progress may be made towards 'normalisation' of internationalisation of curriculum; turning the ad hoc and uneven efforts of a few enthusiasts into the normal expectations and requirements of the organisation. Obviously, the development of organisation-wide systems is necessary for this to happen. However, it is also worth noting that such 'culture-change' cannot be effected by university edict alone, but only through the creative utilisation of the imagination and agency of those who comprise the university. Internationalisation of curriculum should therefore be seen as a dynamic process which, much like the process of internationalisation itself, affords staff and students the opportunity to own the processes of their own learning and knowledge production.

References

Aulakh, G., Brady, P., Dunwoodie, K., Perry, J., Roff, G., Stewart, M. (1997) *Internationalising the curriculum across RMIT University*. Melbourne: RMIT.

Francis, A. (1993) *Facing the Future: The Internationalization of Post-secondary Institutions in British Columbia*. Vancouver, British Columbia: Task Force Report, Centre for International Education.

Haarlov, V. (1997) *National Policies for the Internationalisation of Higher Education in Europe 1985–2000 (Case: Denmark)*. Stockholm: Hogskoleverket Studies, Hogskoleverket Agency for Higher Education.

IDP Education Australia (1996) *Curriculum Development for Internationalisation: Australian Case Studies and Stocktake*. Canberra: DEETYA.

Knight, J. and de Wit, H. (1995) 'Strategies for internationalisation of higher education: historical and conceptual perspectives', in de Wit, H. (ed.) *Strategies for Internationalisation of Higher Education*. Amsterdam: European Association for International Education.

Van der Wende, M. C. (1996) 'Internationalising the Curriculum in Higher Education', in *Internationalisation of Higher Education*. OECD: Centre for Educational Research and Innovation.

13

Internationalisation of the curriculum

Teaching and learning

Dr Betty Leask, University of South Australia

An internationalised curriculum will utilise a wide variety of teaching and learning strategies, all carefully selected and constructed to develop graduates who, as professionals and as citizens, can call on a range of international perspectives. This chapter links with the previous one on institutional approaches, focusing here on 'what is taught/learned' (i.e. on content and outcomes) and on 'how it is taught/learned' (i.e. on teachers' and learners' activities).

What is your purpose?

Why do you want to internationalise your curriculum? Perhaps you are preparing students for professional practice which, in the twenty-first century, means working in a shrinking, multi-cultural and global community. International perspectives required in different professional areas will vary considerably. While practising nurses, pharmacists and engineers should all be able to recognise intercultural issues relevant to their professional practice and have a broad understanding of social, cultural and global issues affecting their profession, the strategies they will need to use to deal with these issues will probably differ. Programmes preparing nurses or pharmacists are more likely to focus on the development of socio-cultural understanding. Those preparing engineers might stress students' understanding of the global and environmental responsibilities and the need for sustainable development. You may choose, for example, to focus on developing intercultural understanding and communication skills in students; on the development of knowledge informed by international research which incorporates a variety of cultural perspectives; on the application of skills and knowledge linked to professional practice in an international, cross-cultural environment; or on a combination of these. Other commonly stated motivations for internationalising include:

- preparation of students for an internationally recognised and accredited examination;
- the development of graduates who can be active and critical citizens;

- catering for the needs of an increased number of international students in classes;
- compliance with university policy.

Establishing your motive (or motives) for internationalisation makes it easier to focus your thinking and to develop clear course objectives. Decisions tend to cascade downwards with motivations for internationalisation influencing objectives at programme and course level, and objectives, in turn, influencing the content and/or methods you select for teaching, learning activities and assessment. All these decisions will be influenced by the nature and needs of your students. So the place to start is with your purpose and once established, you can start to make decisions about both the 'big picture' and the 'fine detail' of the curriculum. The remainder of this chapter focuses on the layers of and participants in the curriculum which together comprise the 'big picture' and the 'fine detail'.

'The big picture': thinking about policy

It may be relevant to consider institutional policies before considering how to internationalise. Policies, often in the shape of mission statements and institutional goals, may be drafted to achieve purposes such as greater cultural diversity within the student and staff community or more culturally inclusive teaching. The practical implications of policy that seeks to drive change will need to be considered as part of the landscape within which you internationalise your curriculum.

'The big picture': thinking about programme

A typology of different types of programme provides a useful starting point for thinking about ways to design and structure a programme, defined as an interconnected number of blocks variously called courses, modules, units, etc. (IDP, 1995, p. 20). (See Table 13.1 on p. 121.)

The categories described in the typology overlap and in practice, any of the features of the typology can operate with others. This mix reflects the complexity of internationalisation and the broad range of options available.

'The fine detail': thinking about the course

There are several layers which together comprise the fine detail of internationalisation of the curriculum. Decisions will be made at the level of the course (with a need to consider how choices influence programme decisions); at the level of the teacher; and when considering students.

It is likely that different decisions will be made about how and how far individual courses will internationalise within an overall programme. For the student the collective experience is what counts. In simple terms a course can be internationalised by any or all of the following:

- broadening the scope of the subject to include international/intercultural content;
- broadening the scope of international/intercultural contact;
- adopting approaches to teaching and learning which assist in the development of intercultural engagement and cross-cultural communication skills.

Often, the overall goal of the above is the development of international and/or intercultural perspectives in students. But what is meant by 'international perspectives'? And how is the development of intercultural perspectives related to internationalisation of the curriculum?

Students' 'international perspectives'

International perspectives may relate to students acquiring special skills or knowledge, allowing them to:

- understand the relationship between a local field of study and professional traditions in other nations and cultures;
- understand how patterns of cultural dominance have influenced the development of knowledge and practice within a discipline;

Table 13.1 Curricula typology and defining characteristics

Curricula typology	Defining characteristics
Prepares graduates for international practice.	• Professional knowledge and practice in the international environment determines content and delivery. • Objectives specify the professions for which they prepare students.
Leads to internationally recognised qualification(s).	• Programme recognised by international accrediting bodies. • Successful completion leads to an internationally recognised professional qualification.
Leads to joint or double degrees in international and language studies.	• Study components combine international/cross-cultural studies with professional studies; conferral of a double or joint degree.
Compulsory parts offered at/by universities abroad, staffed by local lecturers (including exchange and study abroad programmes).	• Part-delivered by another institution in another country. • Part-delivered and assessed using distance methods. • Credit given for prior learning undertaken offshore.

- understand the implications of local decisions and actions for the international community and of international decisions for local communities;
- apply international standards and practices within a discipline area;
- recognise and deal with intercultural issues in professional practice.

Outcomes associated with the development of values and cross-cultural awareness might focus on students':

- awareness of how culture influences their and others' values and actions;
- recognition and appreciation of different cultural perspectives on the same issue;
- valuing of cultural and linguistic diversity and difference.

These kinds of outcomes rely on students being able to relate, interact and function in ways that require meaningful, deep levels of communication and engagement. This is much more than the 'cultural tourism' that is often claimed to be 'internationalisation of the curriculum'. It involves giving careful consideration to the contributions made by others who are seen as culturally different: How have they contributed to the knowledge, assumptions and biases that are built into the discipline knowledge or how have they shaped how these aspects are applied in practice?

Cultural diversity in the classroom

Cultural diversity in the classroom can be one of your greatest resources for developing your own as well as your students' international/intercultural perspectives. But in order to utilise it you will need to create learning tasks that require critical refection on and discussion of how personal attitudes and values are shaped by and reflect cultural values. You, with your students, might explore, for example, how cultural values are reflected in discipline-based knowledge and professional practices. To reap the benefits of diversity, you will need to encourage students to communicate, explore, explain, inquire and negotiate meaning. They will need many opportunities to interact with each other sharing knowledge, ideas and theories from multiple contexts; to explore each other's and their own culture, conceptual systems and values; and to reflect critically on the relationship between culture, knowledge and action within the discipline.

Students can benefit greatly from working together in culturally mixed small groups but the benefits derived are to a large extent dependent on the nature of the tasks that they are set (Volet and Ang, 1998). Merely placing students in mixed culture groups to work on unstructured tasks unrelated to the exploration and sharing of cultural and national perspectives is unlikely to result in the development of international or intercultural perspectives. However, the provision of structured and assessed tasks requiring engagement with different cultural perspectives on a problem or issue, critical reflection on the relationship between culture, nationality and social action or the negotiation of meaning and action across cultural boundaries is more likely to engage students in meaningful international/intercultural learning experiences. (See Chapters 8 and 9 for more on this issue.)

However, cultural diversity in the classroom also presents challenges. In order to provide a relevant educational experience for all students in an environment that is supportive and inclusive of all, you will need to be prepared to review and interrogate your own culture and values. Through reflection, you could consider how your own culture and values influence your teaching practice and, in particular, decisions in relation to selecting content and designing teaching, learning and assessment tasks. This is not straightforward. You will simultaneously need to be outward looking and alert to new input. At the same time you will need to be actively pursuing intercultural engagement with your students and within the discipline and seeking opportunities to learn about the national and cultural perspectives of others. Finally you will need to use this new information to interrogate what is taken for granted in the way your discipline constructs, communicates and acts upon knowledge.

Key course planning questions

The questions shown in Table 13.2 identify aspects to consider when planning how to internationalise your curriculum.

Alignment between the different elements assists the integration of internationalisation across the programme and attention to one or the other elements often requires adjustment in another aspect. However, seeking at least initial answers to the above questions is an important first step in moving towards an internationalised curriculum. Once you have answered these questions it will be necessary to write them down.

Course documentation

Apart from giving a general overview of the course requirements, course documentation provides important scaffolding and helps to highlight areas of importance.

Table 13.2 Internationalising your curriculum: aspects to consider

Outcomes	What international perspectives (knowledge, skills and attitudes) should graduates in this course, at this level, in this professional area develop?
Assessment	What assessment task(s) could students complete to demonstrate achievement of these perspectives?
Content	What international content and/or contact will students need in order to develop these perspectives?
Learning environment	What learning activities and tasks will assist learners to develop these perspectives and prepare for the assessment?
Resources	What resources (including people, online tools) are available to achieve the above?

Statements of course goals, objectives and assessment need to include:

- information on the international perspectives developed and assessed;
- a clear description of the course cross-cultural communication content and skills;
- the international professions for which the course prepares students. This may be stated in the general description and will need to be repeated in specific objectives.

Course content

Thinking about ways in which content can be internationalised is a common way to start making decisions. You might include:

- case studies and examples from different countries and cultures;
- real or simulated instances of cross-cultural negotiation and communication;
- specific reference to intercultural issues in professional practice;
- comparative contemporary international and local content;
- accounts of the historical and/or cultural background to current international practices;
- investigation of professional practices and traditions in other cultures;
- exploration of how knowledge may be constructed differently from culture to culture in the discipline area.

Your planned activities might:

- address issues such as social justice, equity, human rights and related social and economic issues;
- address critical global environmental issues;
- use a recently published, international textbook;
- use and analyse international sources such as journals and conference proceedings.

Teaching and learning activities

A curriculum will become more international if teaching and learning activities require the use of:

- international contacts and networks in the discipline/professional area;
- electronic links and networks, such as email chat groups, with students of the discipline in other countries;
- problem-solving exercises and/or research assignments with an international or intercultural component;
- internships/placements in international or intercultural agencies;

- simulations of international or intercultural interactions;
- presentations or input from guest lecturers with international experience who address specific topics in the course.

Tasks can be constructed that encourage students to:

- explore various value positions and their implications for the field or profession;
- analyse the cultural foundations of alternative approaches to the profession/discipline;
- consider cultural assumptions underlying responses to ethical and social issues related to the discipline/professional area.

Students would inevitably consider issues and problems from a variety of cultural perspectives if you asked them to:

- establish working relationships with fellow students from diverse backgrounds and cultures. Suitable activities might include analysis of media reports from international newspapers, interviews with international students and/or professionals who have worked internationally;
- locate, discuss, analyse and evaluate information from a range of international sources;
- undertake fieldwork with local organisations working on international projects or national projects with an intercultural focus.

Students could undertake reflective writing tasks focusing on international or intercultural matters or explicitly outlining any cultural aspects of thinking processes used in the discipline. Other formats, written and oral, would also be appropriate to assess students' ability to:

- analyse the cultural construction of knowledge and cross-cultural practices;
- compare and contrast approaches to cultural pluralism in different nations and their implications for citizens and for professional practice in the discipline;
- examine ways in which particular cultural interpretations of social, scientific or technological applications of knowledge may include or exclude, advantage or disadvantage people from different cultural groups;
- analyse issues, methodologies and possible solutions associated with current areas of debate within the discipline from a range of cultural perspectives;
- explore cultural and regional differences in values and assumptions affecting the discipline and how these might impact on the actions of individuals;
- explore comparative professional practices and their relationship to cultural values.

Assessment practices

Whereas the previous section suggested what you might assess, this section suggests practices which, in themselves, both check on and encourage internationalisation. Any or all of the suggestions below will be enhanced if you make clear to students how the assessment tasks relate to the development of international perspectives.

Assessment criteria could specify and evaluate cross-cultural communication skills and could explicitly link to international standards. Criteria could be set jointly with students, asking them to self-evaluate their development of international perspectives or to require students to reflect on their own culture as well as engage with that of others.

You could include a range of group and individual projects so that students are assessed for their ability to work with others, to consider the perspectives of others and to compare them with their own perspectives. Activities could be organised in simulated international professional environments or could require students to present information to, and get feedback from, a real or simulated 'international' or cross-cultural audience. Finally, you could set tasks that require students to compare local and international standards in the professional area/discipline.

Internationalisation at the level of the teacher

Because internationalisation is as much about teaching processes as it is about content, teacher preparation and knowledge is an important aspect of an internationalised curriculum.

It is helpful to identify the knowledge and skills that you would like to develop to assist you to internationalise your teaching. Where are the gaps in your knowledge and your teaching skills? How can you address these? Table 13.3 contains a self assessment questionnaire to get you started. It focuses on both what is taught and how it is taught.

Table 13.3: How prepared am I to teach an internationalised curriculum?

Student focus

❏   I know the cultural profile of student groups I teach.

❏   I make an effort to find out about and understand the cultural background of my students.

Knowledge

❏   I am aware of the status of my own professional/teaching area in other educational systems and traditions.

❏   I am familiar with the different theoretical approaches to my discipline used in other systems and traditions.

❑   I understand the international context of my professional area and how my profession has developed in other countries.

❑   I am familiar with international literature in my field.

❑   I can discuss concepts and theories in my professional area from the point of view of other traditions, as well as my own.

❑   I regularly consult with international colleagues.

❑   I can describe how the general features of my professional area are expressed in other countries.

(based on Farkas-Teekens, 1997)

Presentation in lectures and tutorials

❑   I routinely introduce myself and require my students to do the same in tutorials and other small group settings.

❑   I model appropriate cultural awareness and interpersonal behaviour with all students, particularly in small group settings.

❑   I demonstrate that I value diversity of language and culture by my actions and interactions with others.

❑   I regularly talk to my students about what forms of written information they find most useful.

❑   I regularly invite and obtain feedback on my teaching from a representative sample of my students.

❑   I am clear about the difference between a lecture and a tutorial; know what I expect of students in each, and communicate those expectations to students at the beginning of each study period.

❑   I provide (before or during the first lecture) an outline of lecture and tutorial topics/assessment tasks and their sequence for my course.

❑   I structure my presentations clearly and effectively.

❑   I provide a handout outlining the aims, content and structure of each teaching session.

❑   I use clear and concise visual aids to support my teaching.

❑   I ensure that all students can see my face and hear me clearly whenever I teach.

❑   I always try not to speak too quickly and to pause when I have made an important point that requires noting.

❑   I permit/encourage students to tape my lectures.

Presentation of materials

❑   I structure and format written material to be readable and accessible.

❑   Where appropriate, I use illustrations, diagrams, tables and charts.

❑   I use short, clear sentences and address my students directly.

❑   I rarely use idiom or colloquialism in my writing, and if I do use them, I put them into 'inverted commas'.

❑   I provide definitions and glossaries for all specialist vocabulary, abbreviations and acronyms.

❑   I often use headings and sub-headings to signal the structure and plan of written texts.

- ❑   I use dot points and lists to break down complex and interrelated ideas.
- ❑   I routinely ask other people to critique and comment on my drafts.

Assessment practices

- ❑   I require students to seek information from culturally different others and use this information to complete assessment tasks.
- ❑   I require students to work in multi-cultural or multi-national groups for assessment purposes.
- ❑   I provide frequent formative feedback to students early in the study programme.
- ❑   I provide students with choices and options in relation to types of assessment task.
- ❑   I analyse patterns of student assessment completions and results for signs of any difficulties for particular groups of students.

How the teacher him- or herself behaves is an important but often overlooked aspect of internationalisation of the curriculum.

Internationalisation of the curriculum at the level of the student

Both home and international students' perspectives are relevant here but the percentage of each in your class is not. The mere presence in class of international students will not internationalise the curriculum or the experiences of domestic students. In this chapter, you will doubtless have noticed the preponderance of group processes and tasks as these are an integral part of the overall internationalisation goal. Requiring students to work across cultures assists the development of cross-cultural communication skills and understanding on both a personal and a professional level. It also values and includes the contributions of international students, validates the points of view of others and promotes cross-cultural and international understanding.

You may also have noticed that some of the strategies require you to step out of the traditional role of the academic as 'the authority in authority' and learn from the international students in your classes. Thus internationalisation of the curriculum is as much about you as it is about what you teach and to whom.

Conclusion

In this chapter I have focused on what internationalisation means for programmes, courses, teachers and students in higher education, highlighting the depth, diversity and complexity of the issue. There are many possible strategies for achieving a broad range of internationalisation outcomes but all focus on students' international perspectives, nurtured in an environment that is supportive and inclusive of national and cultural difference and diversity.

References

Farkas-Teekens, H. (1997). 'A profile of the "ideal lecturer" for the international classroom'. In H. Farkas-Teekens and M. van der Wende (eds) *Teaching in the International Classroom,* Nuffic papers 8 (Vol. April 1997). Amsterdam: Nuffic.

IDP Education Australia. (1995). *Curriculum Development for Internationalisation, OECD/CERI Study Australian Case Studies and Stocktake.* Canberra: Department of Education, Employment and Training.

Volet, S. E. and Ang, G. (1998). 'Culturally mixed groups on international campuses: an opportunity for inter-cultural learning'. *Higher Education Research and Development,* 17 (1).

14

Postgraduate research

The benefits for institutions, supervisors and students of working across and between cultures

Associate Professor James Sillitoe, Ms Janis Webb, Ms Christabel Ming Zhang[1], Victoria University

Introduction

This chapter discusses Western and Eastern (Confucian heritage) perspectives of research, in particular the benefits of working across and between cultures for research students, supervisors and institutions in social and behavioural science research. Our experience is based in Australia, involves qualitative research in social and behavioural sciences, and focuses on postgraduate students from Confucian traditions. We believe, however, that the conclusions we draw, although tentative, are likely to be more widely applicable. We hope that our comments will stimulate wider interest in the potential of international research students from a range of cultural backgrounds and lead to richer and more insightful research into questions of social importance.

Some thoughts on cross-cultural differences in approach to research

Much has been written about students' different conceptions of learning. Here we turn to a parallel enquiry as to the underlying ideas and conceptions of research in Western and Confucian-tradition contexts. In 2004, we contacted an active research scholar in the Peoples' Republic of China (PRC) and requested a companion statement to the one below we saw as outlining the essence of Western research philosophy:

> The spirit of western civilisation is the spirit of enquiry. Its dominant element is the logos. Nothing is to remain undiscussed. Everybody is to speak their mind. No proposition is to be left unexamined. The exchange of ideas is held to be the path to the realisation of the potentialities of the race.
>
> (Hutchins, 1952)

Our PRC colleague responded:

> The traditional method of knowledge generation was based upon the notion that the order of nature should be used to explain social order and structure.

Hence the three themes, which still underpin contemporary approaches to research, emerged: the harmonious co-existence of nature and humanity; the co-benefit and improvement of nature and society; and the aim of a harmonious and holistic view of the world. Under the influence of western research ideas, Chinese scholars became more analytical, but maintained the traditional holistic perspective on the world.

(Adapted from Zhang, 2004).

The two statements offer, on the one hand, an 'adversarial approach' to knowledge production in the Western context and a more 'consensual' development of knowledge in the Confucian tradition. Students grounded in the consensual tradition, experienced in Confucian culture (which includes their culturally influenced approach to education in general), will probably bring those assumptions with them when arriving at a Western university. We believe that supervisors can help students manifest and extend their assumptions about research in their new, Western context and in doing so, encourage students to contribute to the entire process in novel ways.

Benefits for the generation of knowledge

Qualitative research involves interview, questionnaire, document analysis and participant observation. We have seen how a shared and deep understanding of respondents' experiences builds rapport and deepens the conversation between researcher and respondent, when they share a language. In such interviews, respondents generally used their first language when investigating abstract ideas, feelings and uncertainties. As interviews progressed, 'key moments of exchange' were often marked by a switch from English to first language, thus allowing the interviewer to recognise the incident's importance. Switching to a shared first language also gave the interviewer confidence to pursue culturally sensitive issues.

In this extract, from a study of the adjustment experiences of students, discussion in English is recorded in standard type, whilst discussion which had spontaneously reverted to Mandarin is recorded in italics (I = interviewer, R = respondent):

R: ... because of the great pressure. And my friend taught for about half a year, then she quitted. She said there was great pressure. She also studies [deleted] in here.

I: OK. So pressure, what sort of pressure?

R: She said maybe she taught [deleted] which was the new course in Hong Kong. She had to prepare a lot for the subject. And the school demanded you to prepare well, you had to teach well. *You had to teach students to learn perfectly well. But now the students won't listen. Last year three teachers suicided.*

I: *You mean the respect for teachers and close relationship between teachers and students are no longer there?*

R: *It's different nowadays.*
I: *The world changes fast.* OK, thank you for that.

The gravity of the message may have been overlooked by a less culturally aware interviewer and its significance would not have been clear unless interviewer and respondent shared a common educational background – in this case, of the Confucian *Trimetrical Classics* (Wen, Zhou and Fan, 1994). As the reader may fall into this category, we note that students whose social understandings are drawn from the *Trimetrical Classics* relate to teachers in the following way:

Wen ren zi	As children
Fang shao shi	You are in early stages of life
Qin shi you	Respect teachers and friends
Xi li yi	Learn courtesy and good manners

Thus, the deep respect shown by children for their parents is transferred to their teachers (an obligation for 'upward' respect). There is a reciprocal responsibility for teachers to teach well and accept responsibility for the academic *and moral* success of their students (a 'downward' obligation). In this exchange, both interviewer and respondent share an awareness of blame from both perspectives: students had failed to meet their obligation for upward respect, and teachers had reacted to this by realising their failure to imbue moral standards in their protégés, a circular complex of obligations characteristic of a collectivist culture (Hofstede, 1991). Thus, in exchanges such as the one illustrated, international postgraduate students can contribute to the generation of new knowledge and new insights.

A second, often overlooked, benefit from working with international postgraduate students derives from their tendency to bring a determined attitude and often, a commendable attention to detail to their work. Much research activity involves tedious collation of material, filing of results, and reporting of interviews. Many international postgraduates have background training in repetitive learning (Biggs, 1996), sometimes mistakenly referred to as rote learning, with its emphasis on seeking meaning through returning again and again to the task. This may have a parallel in students' attention to data collection and reporting, seeking understanding of the messages contained in such material.

Finally, international postgraduates may have, through their previous experiences of research and consensual and collectivist values, advantages when considering emerging research areas. For example, sustainability, global warming, loss of biodiversity, and increasing pollution have begun to stimulate a rethink of current economic imperatives. Western students, schooled in adversarial notions and belief in man's supremacy over nature, might find Confucian concepts of holistic principles and respect for the oneness of nature and humanity provide clearer insight into this area of growing importance.

Benefits for the institution

Institutions in general and universities in particular are keen to demonstrate successful outcomes for international research projects. They wish to recruit international research students and scholars, and to develop relationships with international institutions, especially those with commercial interest. We suggest such developments will in themselves engender a new type of researcher schooled in (and therefore acceptable to) Western research tradition but with the ability to penetrate others' cultural practices. Such researchers could contribute to more informed understandings of mutual problems. For example, Lee and Chien (2002) report on a Hong Kong study of pre-operative patient teaching that replicated one in Australia. The principal researcher was able to carry out interviews in Cantonese, transcribe and translate them, and use his familiarity with protocol to gain ethical clearance for the study. Another example of how cross-cultural knowledge can be a vital component of successful research concerns investigating processed food exports from Australia to Asia (Bhaskaran and Irwin, 1995). In such an endeavour, religious requirements, local taste preference, hygiene laws, food handling practices and culinary customs intertwine, necessitating a researcher with knowledge of the local systems. By training international students who might fit this and similar roles, universities are potentially creating a new type of social researcher.

Benefits for the supervisor

With domestic students, the 'how' of research is often never discussed by supervisors. Supervisor and postgraduate student may never get around to matters such as appropriate references for research purposes; whose ideas are reported in the thesis; who a student can talk to about the research; who is responsible for proof-reading and editing the dissertation, and so on. Both sides may avoid these matters because supervisors think that students already know the answers, or because students regard them as inappropriate. However, supervising international postgraduates stimulates a more focused and explicit approach to supervision, often using group discussions where local and international students together consider underlying aspects of the research process. The result is to sharpen and clarify practices for all.

Group discussions also help unearth the meaning of underlying concepts and practices such as what is meant by a 'critical' engagement with a research topic. Supervisors need to make this concept accessible to all students, including those trained in reproduction rather than speculation. Similarly, the group might discuss 'theorising' from empirical data at the PhD level with students trained in both inductive and deductive thinking. As students share their perceptions, issues such as how a thesis writer decides when to explicitly quote from published work, to modify other workers' ideas, or to paraphrase published material will emerge. Ensuring students understand the nuances of difference between these choices is especially important, given the concern about plagiarism. In these and other complex matters, we as supervisors are as much learners as our international students.

A supervisor may need to work sensitively with a student at the start of the process to ensure they form a research question that meets their needs and that brings into play their own perspective grounded in skills, understandings, and 'insider knowledge'. Subsequently, the student usually begins to assume control at the level of data collection and analysis. Finally, whilst the writing of the thesis in formal English prose for university graduation will necessarily involve the supervisor and others in the final dissertation, should dissemination of the findings of the research *into the home culture and language* of the student become important, it is entirely the bailiwick of the student.

Conclusion

What we have tried to present here is an argument for some ways in which international research students can both benefit from, and contribute to, the conduct, collection of data, analysis and findings of social and behavioural science research projects in Australia. Although we have confined our comments to students from a Confucian heritage background, some limited experience we have had with international students from other heritages have hinted at wider possibilities for Australian research in our multicultural society.

Arising from a consideration of the perspectives given in the literature, coupled with our own experience in the area of postgraduate supervision, has arisen a tentative theoretical framework that we have followed in our practice. Simply stated, we have regarded our students' experiences in a different culture as an important base for the development of theories of action in cross-cultural situations, and their facility with a second language being an important research tool enabling the project to more clearly understand nuances and complex meanings that are often poorly appreciated or indeed overlooked from an Australian (predominantly Eurocentric) perspective. We look forward to developing this framework in terms of research into sustainability issues, and in so doing cement the place of this new 'type' of researcher in the overall research capabilities of this country.

Notes

1   We wish to record special thanks to Associate Professor Zhang Yi of the Institute of Public Administration, Guangdong, PRC, for his help in understanding Confucian research culture. In addition, we record thanks to Mrs Tang Liying for supplying the English translation of Professor Zhang's comments.

References

Bhaskaran, S. and Irwin, P. J. (1995). *Review of Market Potential for Indigenous Indian Dairy Desserts*. Rural Industries Research and Development Corporation, Kingston, ACT.

Biggs, J. (1996). 'Western misconceptions of the Confucian-Heritage learning culture'. In D. Watkins and J. Biggs (eds) *The Chinese Learner: Cultural, Psychological and Contextual Influences*. Hong Kong and Melbourne: Chinese Educational Research Centre (CERC) and the Australian Council for Educational Research (ACER).

Hofstede, G. (1991). *Cultures and Organisations: Intercultural Cooperation and its Importance for Survival: Software of the Mind*. London: Harper Collins.

Hutchins, R. (1952). 'The Tradition of the West', in *The Great Conversation: The Substance of a Liberal Education*, Volume 1, *The Great Books of the Western World*. Chicago: Encyclopaedia Britannica, Inc.

Lee, D. and Chien, W. (2002). 'Pre-operative patient teaching in an acute care ward in Hong Kong: a case study'. *Contemporary Nurse*, 13, 271–280.

Wen, Z., Zhou, Z. and Fan, H. (1994). *Trimetrical Classics*. Beijing: People's University Press.

Zhang, Y. (2004). Private communication.

15

Collaborating and co-learning

Sharing the message on teaching
international students within institutions

Ms Lee Dunn, Southern Cross University
Ms Jude Carroll, Oxford Brookes University

Much of this book considers and advocates for decisions made either at the level of the individual teacher, at the level of the programme team or at the strategic level by the institution itself. Graham Webb, summing up Chapter 12 on internationalisation of the curriculum, notes: 'the development of organisation-wide systems is necessary ... however ... such "culture-change" cannot be effected by university edict alone, but only through the creative utilisation of the imagination and agency of those who comprise the university'. This means that internationalisation and effective teaching of international students relies on individual teachers working with colleagues, using opportunities as they arise and creating them when they do not. Some authors (Peters, 1997; Farkas-Teekens, 1997) consider it unlikely or highly unusual to find the broad range of skills necessary to teach international students effectively within one individual. Instead, they advocate team teaching and working in groups. Another reason to collaborate is the need for professional development for teachers of international students, something that is confirmed by own research and that of others (e.g. Dunn and Wallace, 2004; Dixon and Scott, 2003). This chapter considers how you might foster efforts to increase the overall pool of knowledge and expertise within teaching teams, departments or the university as a whole. We focus on professional development and collaboration as this is a significant contributor to better experiences for teachers and all students.

Learning informally about teaching international students

Well-run workshops on teaching international students are a recognised way of enhancing teachers' knowledge and later in the chapter, we offer suggestions on structuring and running them. However, there are other ways in which teachers learn and develop, which complement or even exceed the learning derived from workshops. Much learning happens via national and even international interest groups who focus on international students and in some cases on specific aspects of teaching and learning. In the UK, possible contact points for meeting others with similar interests include UKCOSA: the Council for International Education,

BALEAP: the British Association of Lecturers in English for Academic Purposes, the Learning and Teaching Support Network Subject Centres based in the HE Academy, or SEDA: the Staff and Educational Development Association. In Australia, the Database of Research on International Education maintained by the Australian Council for Educational Research for the Australian Government is an excellent resource, as well as IDP: Education Australia, while HERDSA: the Higher Education Research and Development Society of Australasia will have publications, conferences and networks addressing the issues discussed in this chapter and elsewhere in this book. All these organisations maintain websites with recent activity and contact details.

Another way to reconsider your own practice and to encourage others to develop as teachers of international students is to create a local network. Networks provide a useful setting for review and reflection of practice, for developing new knowledge, and for encouragement and support whilst trying out new practices. Two types are common: institution-wide networks that bring together teachers from different disciplines or roles; and networks formed within a single discipline or departments. The former are usually established and supported by the institution's academic (or learning) development unit and the latter, while there might be some initial involvement from learning developers, are maintained and supported within the discipline or department.

Institution-wide networks can be formed in a number of ways, depending on the institution's culture and overall 'style' though all usually need a recognised body such as the staff development or quality assurance unit to form the network initially and promote its activity. Initial meetings can be scheduled at lunchtime, in late afternoon or even at breakfast. The most important factor is not when they meet or who provides the menu, it is who can be persuaded to attend. Usually, the search for network members starts by identifying people with recognised knowledge and expertise in teaching international students. Your own institution's academic leaders, academic development unit, academic advisers, or international students themselves can all probably provide names. Who is innovative, interesting and even inspiring? Who has a track record of teaching international students effectively? Then the issue becomes finding a format for the first meeting.

We have seen these approaches work:

- Inviting 'good practitioners' to an informal seminar series where each one 'has the floor' for a session. During their allocated session, members can present their own practice, describe others' similar work in the pedagogic literature, or present a problem for joint review. In this case, staff developers organised the network, managed the programme to ensure each session had a leader, and invited new people to join over time.
- Inviting a wide range of teaching staff for an initial meeting with a view to forming a group of those interested in international students. The initial meeting of this network could consist of statements by each member (one or two minutes each) followed by brainstorming and prioritising issues/concerns

to focus the group's future work. In this case, future meetings were managed by the international students office.

- Approaching academic leaders such as Deans or Heads of School to nominate one or more of their staff to form an institution-wide interest group. In this instance, the group came together for the specific purpose of producing a university publication on teaching international students.

Networks based on a single discipline or department can be preferable to and/or complement the more generic ones suggested in the previous section, especially for dissemination of good practice. They are usually formed in similar ways, that is by:

- Approaching specialists, such as those with the departmental role of promoting teaching and learning, and identifying good practice within the discipline or department. This person could then use opportunities such as 'slots' in staff meetings to allow those responsible for the identified practice(s) to share their experiences. An interest-group or informal collaborative relationships could grow as staff see the benefits of learning with and from each other.
- Organising 'paper bag lunch' sessions for experienced teachers of international students to mentor others (perhaps the less experienced), or to allow time and space for teachers to work through challenges and problems they have encountered.
- Inviting a teacher from another department, a member of the academic development unit or a national expert to talk at a staff meeting or lunchtime gathering. This person should be briefed about departmental issues so that the session is targeted and useful. Ensuring the session is not all input but rather has plenty of informal discussion, this approach could stimulate the development of a network amongst those who teach international students.

Supporting networks

Where they are rewarding, useful and fun, networks can evolve into 'communities of practice,' along the lines described by Lave and Wenger (1991) and much cited ever since in the development literature for teachers in higher education. Sharpe (2004) in a chapter entitled 'How do professionals learn and develop?' describes how communities of practice have knowledge of professional practices embedded within them which teachers can access for learning and, in turn, contribute to themselves. Innovation and new knowledge, she notes, are enhanced if staff are taken out of their usual context enough to allow them to see things in a new way yet not so far that they lose the aspects of 'situated learning' that are so vital to making sense of what they learn. A network that functions in this way will need ongoing support and encouragement, including any or all of the following:

- A space to meet. Is there a meeting room (or other space) that could be designated for groups to meet informally? Does it have tea/coffee facilities? Is it welcoming so teachers find a respite from other pressures?
- A convenor who can organise without being too formal or bossy (this role could rotate).
- Help if and when they flounder, preferably from someone with expertise in action research processes.
- Assistance in applying for internal and/or external funding and grants. It also helps to offer feedback if they are not successful, and budgeting or other expertise when they are.
- Institutional 'seeding' grants for improving the teaching/learning or assessment of international students using the resources to buy in research assistance, extra teaching hours or other expertise.
- An outlet for their learning such as reports and articles in newsletters and on appropriate websites.

Once groups or networks are established, online discussion groups can sustain the activity, especially if it is difficult to arrange regular times to meet face to face. However, online discussion forums can fade in the same way that face-to-face networks can diminish without nurturing and support, so it is important for a moderator to be nominated (perhaps on a rotating basis) whose role it is to keep interesting, lively and controversial topics bubbling away online.

Collaborating with specialists

The previous section on networks describes one way in which a range of people concerned with teaching international students might collaborate. A second approach could be to use specialists to add strength and credibility to programmes and collegial discussions. Each institution is likely to have their own specialists (e.g. English language specialists, those who teach study skills, librarians, equity officers, and other student support staff) and there are national and international experts who can contribute their own research. We have experience of online networks where national experts moderated controversial debates about teaching international students. We have brought in writing skills specialists to help our students and valued the immediacy and relevance of the specialist's contribution. We have referred students to counsellors, co-tutored with immigration advisers, sought advice for sticky situations, and used experts to market our courses more widely. We can cite many examples of the smooth interaction of a range of professionals working collaboratively to teach and support international students, each learning from the other in the process. Indeed, the collaborative 'imaginative agency' advocated by Webb as a requirement for internationalisation relies on this sort of co-operation.

Unfortunately, not all teachers have these positive experiences nor are all institutions structured to foster them. In many, staff work on different aspects of the internationalisation project, often in different places and even sometimes with apparently conflicting targets and milestones. We, the authors, have worked in and visited institutions where these groups rarely if ever meet and when they do meet, unless they are careful, they speak in ways their colleagues find hard to understand or value. If you work in a similar setting, then the emphasis is less on learning from each other and more on encouraging better links between specialists or looking for ways that already exist to bring apparently (or real) conflicting views closer together. You could try:

- *Joining relevant project groups.* At the very least, you will better understand others' pressures; at best, you are in the right place at the right time to make your point. For example, we know academics who have joined the cross-university group focusing on Chinese students to ensure the teachers' views are heard and we know recruiters who have asked to attend the next Senior Management Away Day for the Business School so they can influence decisions about student admissions. In most such cases, no one would have thought to invite an 'outsider' along but they welcome the volunteer, even if the role is confined to observer status at first.
- *Encouraging new advocates for international students.* Some forums are typically the domain of academic staff such as the school's annual review or the university's quality assurance committee, but support staff might be able to influence the agenda. If there is already a checklist of matters to be considered, could a case be made for adding a prompt for internationalisation? (This suggestion might be more persuasive combined with the next point about local data.) Academics might do the same by identifying a 'mouthpiece' for their interests in places where marketing and recruitment are discussed.
- *Gathering local evidence to make a case.* Generic or national statistics are less likely to have an impact than those generated from within your own institution. This information may already exist as qualitative data in quality assurance documents or annual school reviews or as quantitative data in the student management system. You might be able to collate and summarise it to make judgements about progression rates, relative rates of failure, or the links between admission requirements and subsequent performance. One colleague commented, 'I was surprised at how the people in the Systems Office welcomed doing a bit of scratching around if you told them why.' If you are not sure what question to ask, colleagues with statistical expertise may be happy to advise.
- *Looking for opportunities for local research.* Many universities have a range of ways to resource small-scale studies or evaluative reviews. They may fund student satisfaction surveys or investigate good questions such as:
  - How do the failure rates compare in different departments or programmes?
  - What are the early signs in this course of students having difficulties with academic study?

- What is the impact of induction on our students' first six months?
- How do national trends match our local ones?

Any conversation between academics and recruiters, for example, would be more fruitful if it included data gathered to answer such questions.

- *Learning others' professional language*, using terms and discourse styles that the other recognises.

Alongside development events that are particularly designed around teaching international students, each institution schedules programmes and activities to enhance knowledge and the practice of teaching as a whole, for example the induction of new teachers or programmes to improve online learning and teaching. Many could (or should) include sessions on teaching international students.

Workshops on teaching international students

Staff developers and experienced teachers or international student advisers are often asked to run workshops on teaching international students. We have been asked to do so ourselves many times as have our colleagues in other universities in the UK and Australia. Our experience, supported by the pedagogic literature (for example, Asmar, 1998; Farkas-Teekans, 1997), tells us there are several aspects in running these workshops in particular, as well as attending to the more general guidance and advice for running all workshops.

All workshops should have an underpinning rationale and scholarship but in the case of workshops about teaching international students, there are several reasons why these aspects need to be made more explicit. As Asmar (1998) notes in a detailed evaluation of a workshop on teaching international students, 'familiarity with the research of others ... should inform and enrich our development activities ... what matters is that our work should be – and should be seen to be – ... academic' (pp. 25–6). However, in this case, research was central to the workshop because many studies contradict commonly held views about international students. Before the workshop, Asmar gathered participants' perceptions of the teaching and learning problems and summarised the five most common perceptions in one column of a table with what she called 'the reality' in the opposite column. For example, she heard teachers and students say that poor English language competence was the main barrier to learning yet Phillips (1993) showed this was not so if the environment is supportive.[1] In the workshop, Asmar set participants the task of overcoming the (mis)perception and maximising the learning potential demonstrated in the research.

The Asmar example also shows the next aspect of effective workshops: gathering information from participants' own situation or institution. For example, in one of our institutions, we used a relatively large-scale questionnaire from the previous year on postgraduates' experiences to structure a session on supporting postgraduate researchers. The participants did insist they spent a great deal of energy in supporting their students and the discussion would have been much less productive without the survey's findings that in the previous year at least, a significant number of students did not *feel* supported. The workshop provided a place where staff could focus on how this might be better targeted, timed and signalled. It is also useful before a workshop to seek out examples of local good practice. Is there an obvious success story? Where are students regularly reporting high levels of satisfaction? What changes in recent years are now embedded and working well? Drawing upon real local examples can be a positive way to encourage participants to review their own practice.

Effective workshops are interactive (Rust, 1998) and interactive workshops take time. Whilst there are many things you might tell participants about teaching international students (such as much of the contents of this book), getting them to take new ideas on board and/or act upon them will probably mean starting with their own experiences, beliefs and deep-seated attitudes. Teachers will need time and encouragement to reflect on what they currently do, share examples of good practice with colleagues, and use their experience to consider specific problems or cases. We have often been asked to address the issue of teaching international students in an hour, in a lecture theatre, or in one memorable case, in ten minutes in a full day devoted to international students' experiences in higher education. If the time allocated is short, you might try to argue for more or alternatively, rethink the agenda in favour of a single, more specific aspect. So, if the question is, 'Can you do it in an hour?', the answer is, 'What do you mean by "it"?' Finally, when planning for interaction, remember that the more diverse the group, the more time you might set aside for them to work in subgroups and exchange ideas and views. Sometimes, participants find this aspect so interesting that presenters can hardly get a word in edgewise, highlighting how seldom participants have the chance to hear about how others address teaching issues.

The next important component of workshops on teaching international students is to link overarching theory and specific good practice recommendations with participants' real problems and issues. People are usually interested in hearing about theories of cross-cultural communication, academic enculturation, culture shock, and learning theories. They often welcome having a theoretical underpinning for recommendations that often seem like common sense. Asmar, in the study mentioned earlier, describes an activity based on using Biggs's cross-cultural 'ladder of abstraction' (cited in its 1997 version). In Asmar's activity, participants worked in small groups using the model to analyse their own practice. Participants often want lists of the key aspects and good practice recommendations such as the importance of being explicit, of focusing on early language issues, of undertaking early diagnosis of students' skills and of providing front-ended support. Then they want time to agree or disagree with these ideas and to consider their own issues.

It is often helpful to identify the specific issues and concerns the group brings with them. These will vary widely and usually cannot be predicted fully though usually, themes mirror the structure of this book. It may take some effort to identify the issues that are significant to all rather than just the more confident and forthcoming or the person with the most power. You then need to pare down the list to something realistic within the time frame. Once you know what you will cover, you can use a range of methods to address them from individual reflection ('Write down what you currently do, how effective it is, etc. etc.') to paired review ('You have five minutes each to tell each other about ...') and small group discussion, either structured around a template or encouraging them to talk and listen to each other. Whatever method you choose, you will need to balance protection and challenge. On the one hand, if people feel attacked or criticised, it will hijack the workshop and prevent them individually or as a group from thinking and changing. On the other hand, you want to challenge and confront issues that must be there or you wouldn't be having the workshop in the first place. There is lots of generic guidance on this in the literature on running workshops and managing conflict.

The final key element to successful workshops in our experience is the inclusion of at least some experiential elements. Workshops that are only theory, only discussion, or only experiential hands-on activities work less well than those that combine all three (Asmar, 1998). One way to include experience is to use exercises that increase participants' empathy with what the international students are experiencing. Here are some ideas:

Empathy exercise 1. Leask (2000, see References) uses a card game exercise where participants divide into small groups, practise a very simple game based on who has the 'top card' in a round and play 'top card wins' until all are confident of the rules (usually about two minutes). One member from each small group then leaves the room whilst the remaining players are given some small variation on the rules (for example, 'even numbers double' or 'face cards don't count'). The newly informed members are told not to share the new rule with the 'outsider' who then returns. Play resumes, the players are all friendly but the newcomer begins to win or lose for inexplicable reasons. He or she usually becomes increasingly confused, frustrated and often begins to withdraw from communication with the others and sometimes from the game itself. The newcomer generally plays slowly, looks worried, etc. It seldom takes more than four or five minutes of this experience before the group has ample material to talk about together, often with lots of laughing yet nevertheless quickly seeing the connection between this activity and international students' experience of their first assessment task. What is it like not knowing 'the rules'? What did each side think of the behaviour of the other? and so on.

Empathy exercise 2. Fluent speakers of a language not spoken by the rest of the group can be asked to address the group for four or five minutes, becoming ever louder and slower with ever more flamboyant hand gestures and mimes. Usually, there is no appreciable improvement in understanding despite these efforts but it can generate reactions worth further discussion. How is it the same or different from the experience of newly arrived international students?

Empathy exercise 3. One of us has developed an essay-writing activity based on a booklet on the history of Ghana written by a Ghanaian with a British PhD which we found in our travels. The author's educational background showed he could present information in a way that was more familiar to UK readers but did not do so in this case. The booklet was 31 pages long and the topic sentence appeared on page 30. (Note: This information is not provided in the exercise itself but provides the template for an experience in writing using someone else's 'rules'.) In the empathy exercise, participants receive an A4 sheet with an 'essay' in ten topic sentences where the language, structure and information mirrors the format expected in a Western university. Participants then are given the template below and must write on the same topic using 'West African rules', usually in about 10 minutes. The template says

> Sentences one to six must describe who the author is, why he or she is suitable for writing this essay or what personal experience entitles the author to address this topic; sentences must not be about the topic itself though the personal information must be linked with the topic, written in the first person and true. Sentences numbered seven to nine must provide background information about the topic and establish the context in which any opinion might be offered. There must not yet be any views expressed about the topic itself but the background must be relevant. The last sentence should hint or imply what the author thinks about the topic, perhaps using a proverb or asking a question.

The result? Most groups struggle with the task and have no idea if they have done it correctly. Many say it 'feels all wrong'. When asked what they would need to find out if the work would warrant a good mark, they usually generate a list of activities that all students would welcome who were in a similar position. They say they want to see some examples and to have further guidance such as what '*personal information*' or '*relevance*' might mean. They want a chance to practise and get some feedback from someone who was good at 'West African writing'. The activity usually takes about 20 minutes and provides ample material that can then be applied to their own teaching.

A different way to include an experiential element in workshops is to bring students' words or even their actual presence into the workshop. We have experimented with many variations on this theme. One of us uses a CD-rom made by the university where students' comments are seen and heard. We've used transcripts of interviews, feedback from focus groups and specially engineered writing exercises such as asking international students at the end of their stay to write a letter of advice to a younger sibling. The students are asked to imagine the recipient is coming to the course next year. What would the student advise them to do to succeed or warn them about potential problems? You can then use extracts to illustrate and support workshop activities.

Actual students, if you can arrange their participation, can make a significant impact. Asmar (1998) evaluated a workshop where three students spoke of their own experiences and interacted with participants on teaching and learning issues five months after the event and found that both students and the teachers spoke of ongoing, positive effects. One professor said, 'For me, the thing that struck me most profoundly were the comments of the students', and then goes on to describe how, after the workshop, 'working with her [the student] has taught me a lot' (p. 24). Arranging for student participation may be relatively straightforward if you have lively contacts with a range of them and know students well enough to select and support those who volunteer. If this is not the case, you could try the Student Union, other teachers, and informal contacts. Panels sometimes are less daunting than a more unstructured format.

A final word about sharing the message

This chapter has discussed a range of ways that teachers individually or working with others can develop and communicate ideas and expertise about teaching international students. None are easy and often, people's expectations and multiple commitments make such activities seem more difficult still. But the good news is that through collaborating, setting realistic goals, attending to what we know about changing the status quo and keeping in touch with others who hold similar views, it is possible to improve your own teaching and the quality of your students' learning.

Notes

1   A 'supportive environment' might be one like the course which a postgraduate student in the UK in 2005 was describing when he said, 'I remember there was one Vietnamese girl who had trouble with her English, but the other people from her region helped her out. I wouldn't class it as a problem; you just got used to how you should talk to her' (*The Guardian*, 19 March 2005).

References

Asmar, C. (1998) 'Scholarship, experience or both? A developer's approach to cross-cultural teaching'. *International Journal of Academic Development*, 4: 1 pp. 18–27.

Dixon, K. and Scott, S. (2003) 'An Examination of the Key Educational Issues to Emerge from a Professional Development Program for Offshore Lecturers in Singapore'. In C. Bond and P. Bright (eds) *Research and Development in Higher Education Vol. 26, Learning for an Unknown Future* (pp. 152–163). Milperra: Higher Education Research Society of Australasia (HERDSA).

Dunn, L. and Wallace, M. (2004). 'Australian academics teaching in Singapore: Striving for cultural empathy'. *Innovations in Education and Teaching International*, 41(3), 291–304.

Farkas-Teekens, H. (1997) 'A Profile of the "Ideal Lecturer" for the International Classroom'. In H. Farkas-Teekens and M. Vander Wende (eds) *Teaching in the International Classroom*, Nuffic Papers 8 (Volume April 1997) Amsterdam: Nuffic.

Lave, J. and Wenger, E. (1991) *Situated Learning: Legitimate peripheral participation*, Cambridge: Cambridge University Press.

Leask, B. (2000). *Teaching NESB and International Students of the University of South Australia, Teaching Guide*. Adelaide: Unversity of Adelaide.

Peters, K. (1997) 'Recruitment and Selection of Lecturers for International Programmes: A case study'. In H. Farkas-Teekens and M. Vandewende (eds) *Teaching in the International Classroom*, Nuffic Papers 8 (Volume April 1997) Amsterdam: Nuffic.

Phillips, D. (1993), *More Than Language*. Video produced by AIDAB/IDP: University of Canberra, Australia.

Rust, C. (1998), 'The impact of educational development workshops on teachers' practice'. *International Journal for Academic Development* 3:1, 72–80.

Sharpe, R. (2004) 'How do professionals learn and develop? Implications for staff and educational development'. Chapter 8 in Baume, D. and Kahn, P. (eds) *Enhancing Staff and Educational Development*. London and New York: RoutledgeFalmer.

16

The student experience

Challenges and rewards

Dr Janette Ryan
Monash University

International students are future ambassadors for not only their university but also for the country in which they are studying. The quality of their learning experience is important for the reputation of the university; for maintaining good relationships in higher education classrooms; and for international students' future careers. Some international students will stay on in the country where they have studied and contribute their skills and knowledge to that country. Most return to their home country and take with them their insights and stories of their time spent overseas. Much of the international student market depends on 'word of mouth' contact with friends and relatives at home. Friendships formed will have lasting personal benefits but the mutual cultural understandings formed will have tangible and intangible benefits for future political, economic and cultural relations between countries across the world.

International students choose to study in another country for a variety of reasons. These may range from the chance of a better career in their home country, the chance of a university place that may be unavailable in their own country, the prestige of a degree from a Western English-speaking country, the perceived opportunity for immigration, or the social and cultural benefits from living and studying in a foreign country. Despite the diversity of these possible motivations, for all international students, the experience is likely to be life-changing. Especially if the study is undertaken while the student is young, and is of several years duration, the experience is likely to be a formative one, and will often change the person's outlook on life and their own concept of themselves, in deeply transformative ways.

Much is at stake for international students. Many will have borrowed from family and friends (perhaps from the local community or village) for this chance at a better life for them and for their family. Failure will have major consequences for their visa status and personal and family finances, as well as the shame of returning home not having achieved success and carrying debts. Students and their parents will also want to know that they have achieved value for money as the annual cost of fees and living expenses will be considerable.

The pressures of higher education study are considerable for any student, but for international students far from home and family and community supports, in often very strange and unfamiliar circumstances, the experience can be overwhelming. International students experience a higher level of mental health difficulties and are at increased risk of attrition, especially in the first year of their studies. The level of support offered to them especially in this first year, and in particular during the first six weeks of their stay, is crucial to their future chances of success. International students have often been amongst the highest achievers in their home country but they are likely to be overwhelmed by the differences they encounter as they struggle to cope with unfamiliar physical, cultural, social and academic environments and conventions. Given the right support and assistance, they will achieve at the same rate as local students, but this will take time and understanding from lecturers and other support staff at universities.

Many universities now have a range of support services available to international students. These include pre-arrival information packages and web-based information, which often provide information on a range of topics through 'frequently asked questions' sections or stories from previous international students. Often different forms of mentoring or buddy systems link newly arrived international students with home students or later year international students. Foundational courses or courses such as English for Academic Purposes are often provided (although not always taken advantage of by international students). International student advisers or international student offices provide support services such as assistance in opening bank accounts and social activities, academic support services, and a range of orientation activities. Many international students arrive late, however, in an attempt to reduce costs, and may miss out on important orientation information. This can be made available in written form prior to arrival which gives students more time to translate and digest the information. It is important that the availability of support staff and services is widely disseminated to international students, as well as academic staff, who can often play a role in, for example, connecting students with an academic skills adviser or learning or language skills unit for more specific academic assistance and support.

Lecturers can do much in this transition period to ensure that the student feels connected and accepted, and so that the load that the student is trying to cope with is lightened as much as possible in this early period. International students will succeed; they may just take longer and, at least initially, need more support. The role of lecturers is to 'bridge the gap' for students to ensure that they understand the new situation and its expectations, and so that international students are given the support necessary for their best chance of success.

Regardless of country of origin or previous level of academic success, international students will experience some degree of loss of self-esteem and self-concept. Home students have had at least eighteen years to learn the behaviours and knowledge that are assumed as 'taken for granted' in higher education learning environments. Simple things such as who should speak in lectures or tutorials, and for how long and in what form, act in subtle ways to shape how people's contributions are encouraged, shared and acted upon. International students may have difficulty in knowing how to participate, and may lack the language facility to express their ideas or be understood, or display their level of under-standing (or misunderstanding). In a lively tutorial, it takes much courage even for a home student to participate and have one's views listened to and valued. For many international students, such environments are alien and discomforting. In many cultures, silence and harmony are valued rather than critical and adversarial discourses and practices.

Lacking language facility can make international students feel as though they have lost their personality and their sense of self as without language it becomes impossible to express any sophistication of thought. Home students often are not willing to make the effort to make friends with international students when the conversation may be difficult. Many international students report that it can take up to a year to make friends with local students, yet such friendships are vital for practising English, learning the culture and feeling accepted. International students are sometimes the subject of racial discrimination and abuse, from home students and sometimes lecturers. They can be aware that they are 'cash cows' for the university and sometimes feel that their presence is unwelcome. They are sometimes shunned by local students in class and especially in the formation of groups for assessed group work as home students may fear that their mark will be dragged down by them.

Most international students are likely to experience three levels of shock. The first is *culture shock*, where the physical environment, food, transport, accommodation, personal relationships, dress and even odours are different and can take some time to get used to. Even simple things such as catching a bus or buying food can be difficult and distressing. They are usually far from friends and family with whom to recount the experience, who will understand their anxiety and provide support and encouragement. This period can be a very painful one, and international students talk about doing things like spending a long time in the shower just so that they have a place to cry in private. Often simple misunderstandings, if not addressed early, can escalate in ways that can have drastic consequences for international students. Home students and lecturers can misinterpret the actions of international students as flaws in character or manners which in fact are the result of different cultural norms. International students can react to the intense frustration and pressures either through sudden anger (often aimed at an innocent party such as a librarian) or sometimes by withdrawal, further alienating those around them. Many international students can recount situations where they have misunderstood a situation and acted entirely inappropriately. They may laugh about this later, but it can be extremely embarrassing at the time (and not at all funny).

The second level of shock is *language shock*. Even for native English speakers, the type of language spoken in conversation, local accents, and the speed of spoken language can be difficult. For non-English speakers, even many years of English language study often ill-prepares them for the realities of everyday spoken language and academic, discipline-specific language. They will have learnt a different kind of English, which has usually been spoken in a clear and standard

American accent. In this early period, students can struggle to understand even 10 per cent of what they hear. They may arrive with an idea of themselves as having very good English. They may have studied English for many years, have been able to speak English well in their English language classes and communicate easily with other English-language learners. They may have achieved a high IELTS score, but this will not have prepared them for the speed, the type of words and expressions used in popular and vernacular language, or the background cultural knowledge embedded within much of what is verbally exchanged. In addition, they will be having to deal with copious amounts of written materials. A conservative estimate of the extra time it takes non-English speaking international students to read and translate written materials is fourfold. Add to this the discipline-specific language used in most higher education courses, and the cognitive (and emotional) load can easily become overwhelming. In such circumstances, many international students will seek out opportunities to talk with others in their own language purely as a tension release, as they can express themselves freely without the constant strain of having to think about the language they are using.

The third level of shock is *academic shock* where different approaches to teaching and learning become apparent to the international student. Many international students report early difficulties with language but that this gives way over time to difficulties with different academic traditions and expectations. This may involve different approaches to the relationships and roles of teachers and students, even for students who come from English-speaking countries. The formality of the relationship and the independence of the learner can be very different. The nature of academic discussion and analysis can vary between Western individualistic, adversarial conventions (of questioning and critiquing) and more holistic, harmonious and collectivist views of knowledge and learning. For many international students, this means that a lifetime of learning has to be 'unlearnt' and a new set of often subtle and mysterious ways needs to replace this. If the demands of the new learning situation become overwhelming, international students will resort to the necessary means to survive, often through (intentional or unintentional) plagiarism, or by resorting to their usual forms of support by banding together and working in groups (often seen as 'syndication' or 'collusion' and therefore cheating). In addition, they can feel alienated by implicit messages that Western ways of scholarship are universal or even superior.

Many international students, however, relish the opportunity to learn new ways, and this is implicit in their decision to study in a foreign country. Many talk about the personal transformation that this provides. For lecturers, however, this means understanding the enormity of the challenges facing international students and their own role as guides in this process.

For most international students, what they most desire is understanding and support. Many of the contributors to this book have themselves been international students and understand just how difficult it can be. Most international students will say that it is the most difficult thing that they have ever done in their lives but also the most enjoyable thing they will ever do. For lecturers too, teaching international students can be the most challenging aspect of their work, but also the most rewarding as they see the enormous effort their students make and the success and sense of achievement that results as life chances are transformed. Intercultural communication and friendships achieve results that last a lifetime.

For Western universities, the international student market is a volatile one. At a purely pragmatic level, it is important that it is done well so that there is no damage to universities' reputations and budgets. For the individuals involved, much is at stake but much is also to be gained. There are potential benefits for everyone: universities, lecturers, international students and home students. Universities have a vital role to play in ensuring that the potential of globalisation works in positive ways and so that the increasing changes to universities are shaped in ways that have positive outcomes for all. Universities, as they always have done, can play an important role in responding to these challenges in ways that bring the best traditions of the great civilisations of the world together in new and dynamic ways.

Index

An environmentally friendly book printed and bound in England by www.printondemand-worldwide.com

PEFC Certified

This product is
from sustainably
managed forests
and controlled
sources

www.pefc.org

PEFC/16-33-415

MIX

Paper from
responsible sources

FSC® C004959

FSC
www.fsc.org

This book is made entirely of chain-of-custody materials

#0167 - 120412 - C0 - 234/156/9 - PB